RESPONSIVE
WEB DESIGN
with **Adobe Photoshop**

DAN ROSE

Adobe

Responsive Web Design with Adobe Photoshop
Dan Rose

Adobe Press books are published by Peachpit, a division of Pearson Education.

For the latest on Adobe Press books, go to www.adobepress.com. To report errors, please send a note to errata@ peachpit.com.

Adobe Press Editor: Victor Gavenda
Development Editor: Stephen Nathans-Kelly
Production Editor: Maureen Forys, Happenstance Type-O-Rama
Compositor: Cody Gates, Happenstance Type-O-Rama
Technical Editors: Dennis Kardys and Joel Baer
Copyeditor: KimWimpsett
Proofreader: Kim Wimpsett
Indexer: Jack Lewis
Cover Design: Aren Straiger
Interior Design: Maureen Forys, Happenstance Type-O-Rama

Printed and bound in the United States of America

ISBN-13: 978-0-134-03563-5
ISBN-10:   0-134-03563-1

9 8 7 6 5 4 3 2 1

Acknowledgments

This book was guided by the resourcefulness of Victor Gavenda, the eagle eye of Stephen Nathans-Kelly (and the Adobe Press team), and the sage wisdom of Dennis Kardys. My gratitude to Dan Mall for trailblazing the Photoshop-for-RWD path. My love and dedication to Amanda for her support and encouragement, to Holly and Norah for play and snuggle breaks, and to Jesus, with whom all things are indeed possible.

Contents

1

PHOTOSHOP'S NEW GROOVE

"We need to make this responsive."

Whether you consider yourself a web design noob or pro, this declaration is as exciting as it is terrifying. Having some experience making responsive sites affords you only a small advantage over those who are just learning how. The way we design, even responsively, has evolved significantly in just two short years. That's the nature of the ever-changing Web, where the best tool you can have in your box is an eagerness to stay as up-to-date as possible.

That's why you picked up this book, isn't it?

At this moment, odds are you find yourself in a dilemma. *Responsive web design* (RWD) is becoming synonymous with simply web design, yet your process hasn't quite caught up. You've always used Photoshop, but its place in a responsive workflow seems a bit forced. *Do I really need to make that many comps? Are any of these newfangled design apps worth trying? There's got to be a better way!*

Even if you've done the responsive song and dance a few times, Photoshop most likely is no longer the workhorse of your web design workflow. Designing solely in the browser continues to pillage would-be Photoshop users, and new apps such as Reflow, Webflow, and Macaw present increasingly viable alternatives. The voices calling for the demise of Adobe's flagship app in web design are well-documented, and it's starting to make sense. You just might be the only one you know who still uses Photoshop for web design. Perhaps it's time to cut your losses and jump ship.

Yet there you are, still reading a book with "Photoshop" in the title. Stubborn. I like that about you.

Called Into Question

Photoshop is the one of the most polarizing topics among web designers today and has been ever since RWD came on the scene in 2011. I can remember the first time I really noticed it, back in September 2012. While scrolling through my Twitter stream I saw a link to a post on Treehouse's blog, titled "Responsive Web Design in the Browser Part 1: Kill Photoshop" (see **Figure 1.1**). Mind you, up until that point, I was already designing responsively but had no idea I wasn't supposed to be using Photoshop anymore.

Figure 1.1 The alternatives seem to be many, but the call to action from the design community seems to be clear: Kill Photoshop!

Now, I'm not easily dissuaded by one person's opinion, but the topic seemed to hit a fever pitch soon thereafter.

▶ "Has Responsive Web Design Killed Photoshop for Web Designers?" (*www .boagworld.com/design/has-responsive-design-killed-photoshop-for-web-designers/*)

▶ "Is Photoshop Dead?" (*www.webdesignerdepot.com/2013/02/is-photoshop-dead*)

▶ "Photoshop Users: How to Switch to Sketch" (*http://blog.mengto.com/ photoshop-users-how-to-switch-to-sketch*)

▶ "Khoi Vinh on Using Sketch Instead of Photoshop" (*www.creativebloq.com/ khoi-vinh-using-sketch-instead-photoshop-6133901*)

▶ "Photoshop Killer" (*www.photoshopkiller.com*)

The next thing I knew, I couldn't find more than a handful of designer friends who said they still used Photoshop, or were willing to admit it anyway. They'd moved onto "more efficient" methods like using Sketch (*www.bohemiancoding.com/sketch*) or just designing with Hypertext Markup Language (HTML) and Cascading Style Sheets (CSS). It's possible you may work somewhere that mandates you use Photoshop. But for designers like myself who have autonomy to use whatever tools and more or less processes they want, dumping a product I've used for my entire career wasn't a trivial matter.

For the past few years, I've tried to find out as much as I can about why the switch from Photoshop is happening and who might still be using it. In my quest I've found a common concern shared by designers: Beyond it simply being a preference, Photoshop is intrinsically tied to their current employment. In other words, when some designers hear "They're telling us to stop using Photoshop," they internalize "I'm worried about my role on the team and potentially my career." That seems pretty heavy for one tool, but don't underestimate the impact it's had on our industry.

Should you switch?

Stick in the Mud

Sure, you could ditch years of Photoshop familiarity, training, and cost. You could invest in a new web design app and never look back, at least until an even newer app comes out. Nobody would blame you, and they'd probably applaud you because you did it in the name of responsive web design efficiency. Everybody is doing it.

Still, I contend that jumping ship because of popularity isn't good enough, not when the other option is simply trying harder to see the redeeming qualities of Photoshop and whether a better process is just a few tweaks away. I have a hunch you feel the same. That's good because we're about to take a deep dive into exploring how to get the most out of Photoshop without sacrificing workflow efficiency.

Fear of the Unknown?

I don't think reluctance to drop Photoshop comes from being afraid to try new tools. I've tried a bunch of them. The appeal is there, and I encourage you to assess them for yourself. Fluid canvasses, adjustable breakpoints, and easy browser previews aren't native to Photoshop. We can hope that these features will be baked in at some point, but that doesn't seem likely. Adding them would require a major pivot from the iconic landscape of the product and likely frustrate users who are just fine with the current canvas.

However, the supposed "lack" of those features makes Photoshop a great environment for designing a single "moment." Designing individual instances, in moderation, can help spur ideas to be introduced on a larger scale. Not everything about designing in a static medium is as bad as you might think. Granted, a lot of new tools have parallels to Photoshop in terms of drawing shapes and placing type. However, when handled appropriately, focusing on a single breakpoint can bring focus to a design. When I don't have to be concerned about what shape navigation takes at a narrower or wider view, I can commit to exhausting an idea.

Can I Still Get by Without Knowing Code?

Equally important, this isn't an "anti-design in browser" cookbook for getting around knowing how to code either. Being able to design in the browser is essential when it comes to responsive web design, and this book has a whole chapter about it. I'm a staunch advocate of designers who can craft HTML & CSS because the structure it provides creates both possibilities and constraints for your design. The benefits aren't just individual, either. Ben Terrett of Gov.UK puts it this way:

> **"**All of the designers can code or are learning to code. We call ourselves the design team because it's important to belong to a group with shared skills and experiences. This helps people develop their skills, support each other, and build a strong culture with shared standards.**"**

> — BEN TERRETT (*https://gds.blog.gov.uk/2014/07/18/whats-the-design-process-at-gds*)

Don't worry, though. If you're a bit behind on your coding skills, there are wonderful resources to help you learn, like Treehouse (*www.teamtreehouse.com*), Code School (*www.codeschool.com*), and Codeacademy (*www.codeacademy.com*) to name a few. I won't be covering anything overly technical, but being able to bring your ideas to life in the browser has never been more critical (see **Figure 1.2**). (If not for lack of resources, what might be holding you up from learning some basic HTML & CSS?)

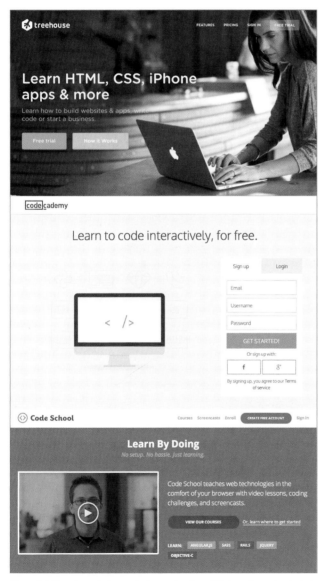

Figure 1.2 The chasm between design and coding skills has plagued web design for years and still exists for many.

So if you're amenable to learning new tools and designing in the browser, what keeps pulling you back to Photoshop? For me, it's a tool I'm just too proficient with to abandon at the arrival of responsive web design. Proficiency is, and always will be, valuable to web design. And before you go disqualifying your own proficiency, note that I only recently got the Save for Web keyboard shortcut down (otherwise affectionately known as Save for Web Claw...just Google it). Proficiency isn't just about knowing your way around; it's about being able to ideate and render your design intent to the best of your ability. So, I'm declaring that it's OK to be a stick in the mud about this one, as long as you're open to figuring out how Photoshop's role is changing.

More Process Than Tool

Because there's no Convert to Responsive button in Adobe Photoshop (see **Figure 1.3**), we're going to have to talk about process a whole lot more than the new bells and whistles in Photoshop CC. (It would be pretty lame if there were such a button anyway.)

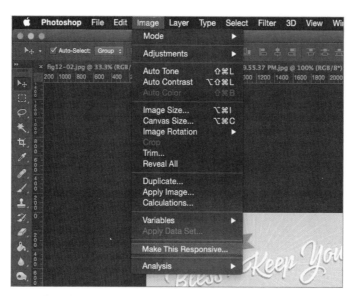

Figure 1.3 Have you found the magic button yet? It appears when you hold down every key except ~ on your keyboard. OK, I'm kidding...don't do that.

I've always maintained the most enjoyable part of web design is creative investigation. Designing for myriad screen widths provides ample opportunity for exploration, and while it often seems like a lot of work, it's work that shouldn't be automated. Each site design presents a set of challenges and problems to solve, and you can spot "templated" solutions from unique and well-considered ones. Design thinking and design tools need to work in beautiful choreography. To make your responsive workflows successful, you need to shift your focus from "Which tool should I use?" to "Where does it make sense to use each tool in my process?"

Today's workflows are about staying nimble. I'm confident you can stay nimble using Photoshop, but you may need to rework your traditional approaches to do so.

A Battle of Two Short Words

I almost made a horrible mistake naming this book.

I was *this* close to titling it *Responsive Web Design in* Adobe *Photoshop*. You just checked the cover to see what the difference is, didn't you? But the distinction may not be clear or significant to you at the moment.

What's the difference between *Responsive Web Design in Adobe Photoshop* and *Responsive Web Design with Adobe Photoshop*?

Distinguishing *with* from *in* is vital. For years, designers have used Photoshop as a program to do web design "in," in its entirety. The "Photoshop phase" of a project was half of the work. Once our infamous "Home.psd, Landing.psd, Interior.psd" mock-ups were approved, we'd wipe our hands clean and move on. Months of project timelines were spent assessing work done in Photoshop.

That was when we were designing for a single screen, and even then you could argue how inefficient and inaccurate of an approach it was.

Designing for multiple screens places greater emphasis on staying nimble. You've probably already experienced how backlogged a project gets when you're making three templates at three sizes each. How about more than ten templates at more than five different sizes? Overwhelming. No doubt you're under the gun to shorten the Photoshop phase, or perhaps you're just genuinely interested in a more efficient method. Logically, if you're cutting down design time in Photoshop, you have to increase the time you spend in HTML & CSS. The trick, as you'll discover, is continuing to work "with" Photoshop even after you (or a developer) start toying with code.

Responsive web design isn't something you can do inside the silo of Photoshop. You can, however, use Photoshop alongside the browser (and a bevy of other tools) to help you design responsively.

Not on the Menu Tonight

Now is as good a time as any to discuss some of the topics I won't be covering in depth, don't you think?

The Core Tenets of Responsive Web Design

On the RWD side, I'm assuming you're familiar with its core tenets: media queries, flexible grids, and fluid images and video (see **Figure 1.4**). Therefore, we won't be spending time defining what's already been so brilliantly defined by the inimitable Ethan Marcotte (*www.alistapart.com/article/responsive-web-design*). He also published the penultimate book on the topic, *Responsive Web Design* (*www.abookapart.com/products/responsive-web-design*). If you haven't read it, do so on my recommendation and that of every other person who owns it.

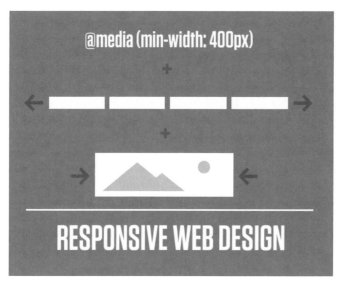

Figure 1.4 RWD = Media Queries + Flexible Grids + Fluid Images. Got it? Good.

Responsive Patterns

There are a ton of responsive patterns and conventions that the fine people in our industry continue to develop, and it would be nearly impossible to detail them in the scope of this adventure. For example, the number of patterns available for navigation at different screen sizes spans from stacking items vertically to triggering an off-canvas menu like Facebook of yesteryear. I'll touch on a little of that, but a much more comprehensive resource I often use Is This is Responsive (*http://bradfrost. github.io/this-is-responsive*), curated by one of the finest people on the Web (and IRL), Brad Frost.

Performance

Lastly, there's a critical component to responsive web design that we designers tend to overlook at our own peril: performance. Some of the most gorgeous sites not only take forever to load on a standard mobile connection but also end up sending your data plan overage fees through the roof. Why is this? Among other things, uncompressed images are to blame, but there are a ton of other factors for slow performance that are a bit too technical for our discussion. Scott Jehl's *Responsible Responsive Design* (*www.abookapart.com/products/responsible-responsive-design*) tackles the impact of the choices we make.

Photoshop Basics

On the Photoshop side, I'll assume you're familiar with the interface. You've comped websites with it, and you more or less enjoy using it. In fact, I'm banking on you loving Photoshop so much that you're reluctant to give it up. For those reasons, I won't be covering the basics of web design in Photoshop, such as how to create buttons by drawing rounded rectangles. That doesn't mean I'll always be talking in advanced terms, but I'll focus on practical applications, rather than the basics.

The Minutiae of Version Disparity

Subsequently, your familiarity with Photoshop may be relegated to a certain version. My hope is that you're on the latest version (CC 2014 as of this writing), but I realize there are several reasons why that might not be the case for you. I do advocate joining Adobe's Creative Cloud. I was a bit skeptical when I heard Adobe was switching to a subscription-based model but have found the benefits considerable. Always using the latest version cuts down incompatibility, pain points, and the fear of missing out on something (or FOMO, as the millennials say). Rest assured, 90 percent of what you'll read in this book isn't particular to the latest version. When it is, I'll do my best to call out CC 2014–only features.

The Merits of Comparable Tools

There's one elephant in the room I want to address, and that concerns the Photoshop skeptics. If you have your doubts that Photoshop is as good of a tool as, say, Sketch,

Fireworks (R.I.P., 2013), or Microsoft Paint, I won't be tearing down those apps in an effort to build Photoshop up.

I don't speak from a lack of confidence in Photoshop; Photoshop is a fantastic web design tool. You might prefer a different app, and that's totally OK; you'll find enough relevant parallels in the coming chapters. But let it be known that I use Photoshop because it works for me, and I in no way prescribe that all web designers need to use it. I will, however, accept the challenge of proving Photoshop as a viable choice for web design (see **Figure 1.5**).

Figure 1.5 Photoshop is my web design tool of preference, and I'm guessing it's yours as well.

Finding Photoshop's Groove

As we set out to write Photoshop's new story, my hope is that you'll come away with some incredibly practical strategies for leveraging it. One of the most important things I've learned in repurposing Photoshop is that an approach might work for one project yet be ineffective for another. Suffice to say, this is all about you being able to discern when, how, and why to use it. That's what I like to call finding Photoshop's "groove."

We were once taught to use Photoshop for a specific task: creating full-page comps. In the next chapter, I'll shoot some holes in that process and discuss some disadvantages that you've heard about or experienced for yourself. While Photoshop is historically synonymous with full-page comps, it's important to distinguish between the two. All those folks advocating for Sketch, Fireworks, and the others are still making comps, too. It's not so much the tool that's faulty but the workflow.

So, where does that leave Photoshop? To keep it in the fold, you'll need to be clever about where it fits with designing in the browser. Some designers are amazing at using code to express design. I am not one of them.

Fortunately, there are a few exercises you can do in Photoshop that are much shorter in scope than full-page comps *and* allow you to work with the browser. That's where I'll spend the majority of the book and from which you can discern which ones are best suited for your workflow. You may have heard of visual inventories, style tiles, style prototypes, and element collages. I'll dissect the best parts of those and introduce some techniques for using them after you have some components started in the browser.

In addition, I've compiled a list of enough plug-ins and extensions to constitute a small nation. I know it's easy to get wrapped up in process, workflow, and deliverables without feeling like you have anything to download or install. I've read more "Top 100 Photoshop Plugins for Web Designers" posts than anyone should ever have to, and I've plucked out the most practical ones I've either used or plan on using. I dare you not to find one worth trying yourself.

By the time you're done this book, you'll be a well-mannered designer after I break down what it means to have "Photoshop etiquette." If you're laughing at the prospect of properly naming and organizing your layers, odds are there's someone who inherits your PSDs and wants to cause you harm but hasn't said anything. Yet.

Anti-full-page comping. Designing with the browser. New-age "deliverables." A jackpot of resources. Some good ol' fashioned etiquette. That's our road map, so buckle up.

We Need to Make This Responsive!

It's crunch time. It's been crunch time for the past few years. Responsive isn't so much an option as a necessity these days, and it's on you to nail it. The only thing that stands between you and a more sensible workflow are the pages that follow.

But before we can get anywhere, we need to understand how our industry arrived at such an unpopular view on Photoshop. Without fully understanding the pain points in using it, we can't be innovative in dodging them.

Let the Photoshop bashing begin!

2

HOW DID WE GET HERE?

The year 2001 was the year I used Photoshop for the first time. I was just one of some 20-odd teens sitting in Mrs. Borges' electronic design class in a rural Connecticut high school. I'm fairly confident my maiden Photoshop voyage was designing a CD cover for my self-titled album, *Rapmasta D*. Let's just leave it at that.

What is worth recalling is how vividly I remember the Photoshop 6 startup screen. The image was a goldish collage of a starfish, a floating eye, and some leaves. Chances are you have fond memories of the splash screen, toolbar, or application icon for the version you learned on too (see **Figure 2.1**). Although most of us can't recall the first version of most software we've used, there's something about Photoshop that tattoos itself on our minds. I suppose it's always been the iconic design program, and today you'd find little argument against that claim.

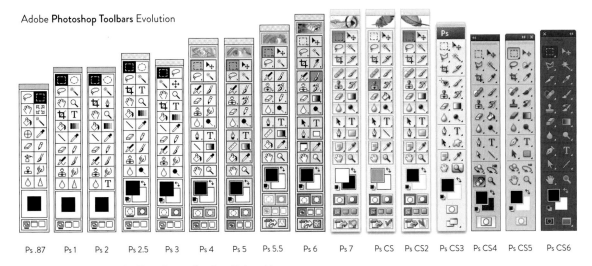

Adobe **Photoshop Toolbars** Evolution

Ps .87 · Ps 1 · Ps 2 · Ps 2.5 · Ps 3 · Ps 4 · Ps 5 · Ps 5.5 · Ps 6 · Ps 7 · Ps CS · Ps CS2 · Ps CS3 · Ps CS4 · Ps CS5 · Ps CS6

Figure 2.1 Everyone knows the Photoshop toolbar from their rookie year. SOURCE: DESIGNMODO

How We Used to Know Photoshop

There's a funny thing that happens when I talk about learning on Photoshop 6. It's not very long before someone chimes in that they started with Photoshop 5. Another interjects, "4!" Then there's the person who matter-of-factly comments, "I've been using Photoshop since it came out and have the floppy disk to prove it." You know the person. Everyone knows that person. Our own version of adoption has become something of a merit badge. No doubt you've had similar conversations or know someone who can "trump" your Photoshop history.

Web designers exhibit an undeniable pride about how long they've been using Photoshop, more so than any other tool and possibly any browser. It's this pride that's sparked an uncanny fandom. Photoshop-related fridge magnets, pillows, mugs, and tons of other doodads have adorned workstations over the past 20 years. Heck, you know you're a Photoshop fangirl when you get the toolbar tattooed to your forearm (see **Figure 2.2**).

Figure 2.2 Impressive dedication (though difficult to update)
SOURCE: BLOGS.ADOBE.COM

Most of us "grew up" as web designers by honing our Photoshop skills. It's not that there weren't alternatives; then-Macromedia Fireworks and Corel Draw had followings of their own. But by and large, the preferred software of design practitioners and educators was Photoshop. Web design curriculums were often structured around teaching its fundamentals.

Quite simply, Photoshop has historically been seen as an integral part of web design by those both inside and outside the industry.

That's what makes the recent falling out of favor so interesting.

The Faults of Traditional Photoshop

After you start Photoshop, what's the first thing you do? For most of us, it looks something like **Figure 2.3**.

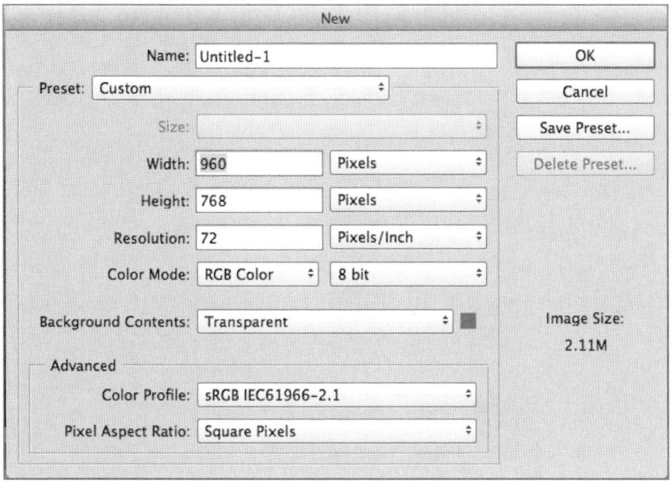

Figure 2.3 960px was a way of life pre-RWD.

Prior to responsive web design (RWD), we made many reasonable assumptions about how our site would be viewed. Most likely, someone was viewing it on a desktop monitor with a resolution of 1024×768. They were using a mouse. Their experience wouldn't start or continue later a smaller mobile device. And so, with that relative confidence, our new document's width was 960px (allowing a little breathing room with 32px of padding on both sides of the screen).

Perhaps you still use 960px as a starting point. What do you do when the viewport gets smaller? Or bigger? The Web should be adaptable to any and all sizes, a concept introduced by John Allsopp in "A Dao of Web Design" (*www.alistapart.com/article/dao/*) in 2000 and reinforced by the mobile device explosion in recent years.

The ubiquity of the Web amplifies the absurdity of entering dimensions for a new document in Photoshop. And if we dig a little deeper, the root of the problem lies in what we set out to create in Photoshop: a brief snapshot in the continuum.

On Full-Page Comps

The most significant change in the way I've used Photoshop over the past few years has been to stop making full-page comps. I define a full-page comp as a mock-up of one page at one size. A prime example would be a homepage comp at 960px. It's a practice many of us have employed for years, and surprisingly, lots of us still do. In a poorly contrived Twitter poll, I found that 72 percent of designers use full-page comps in their RWD process. That majority suggests one of two things: Mock-ups remain a completely viable exercise, or 72 percent of designers have yet to embrace a more sensible workflow.

I tend to believe the latter.

Where Full-Page Comps Made Sense

Let's go back to why this method made sense pre-RWD. In a typical design workflow, someone (usually, but not always, a designer) would create a set of wireframes. Because wireframes often lacked any style considerations, there was a need for a deliverable that acted as a bridge to the development of the site. The next logical step would often be to create a "desktop"-width Photoshop document based on the wireframes, complete with all the intended styles. The set of PSDs would consist of just a few pages (homepage, landing, and interior) or the whole lot. I can see you nodding your head, as if you're all too familiar with this process.

The primary goal of these full-page comps was simple: to get client approval. In doing so, the design team was authorized to continue developing what they'd mocked up while the client had reasonable confidence looking toward the finished product. The result was a complete bridge from wireframe to development, meaning the project could move forward. Mock-ups provided an answer to the all-important question of what the website would look like without ever needing to write a line of HTML & CSS. Conversely, the environment of Photoshop can be conducive to adding detail at the cost of hours, weeks, and months.

A secondary goal of design based on mock-ups is to establish design intent for the development phase. Much like blueprints outline the house plan for a contractor to follow strictly, PSDs are often regarded as equivalent to front-end developers. *Did you measure the padding within that button? Are you using the right blue for the headings? Did you export the repeating background image?* Developers can find all of these answers by referencing the all-encompassing PSDs done at the beginning of the project.

Where Full-Page Comps Go Horribly Wrong

Suffice it to say that the practice of design based on mock-ups enabled two things in regard to communication: the noncoding designer and the "throw it over the wall" workflow.

Let's tackle the code-averse designer first. The Photoshop environment provides a safe haven for those not wanting to test the coding waters. Think about it: You can spend a significant amount of time detailing what a website should look like without ever needing to worry about how it actually functions, whether it breaks in older browsers, or whether renders your type poorly. Surely my sarcasm isn't lost on you.

Fundamentally, code is the language of the browser, and the browser is the environment where your design lives. Even if we're just assessing one screen width, how it functions, breaks, and renders should each be reason enough to become more familiar with how code works and is supported (or not). The issues are compounded only when we start to account for multiple screen widths. No longer can we blindly design sites without knowing how they'll translate to dozens of browsers and hundreds of devices. Producing comps in Photoshop, which is neither a browser nor a device, doesn't give us much insight into this matter.

The second egregious act of full-page comping is what's commonly referred to as the *waterfall* method. This typically starts with a team member creating static wireframes and passing them along to a designer, who makes a mock-up and then sends it down the line to a developer to code. This is referred to as "throwing it over the wall," which is sometimes literally the case in a cubicle setting. I've always thought that there's an incredible collaboration opportunity missed here. Instead of the developer providing programmatic insight that might affect the design *while* it's being created, the developer receives a facsimile to reproduce in code *after* it's done, approved by the client, and not expected to change. The emphasis should be on the importance of a designer *and* developer being part of all phases of a project, especially when so many screens and devices are involved.

One Size Does Not Fit All

Having touched on internal communication, let's shift gears to how we discuss full-page comps with our clients. To deliver a mock-up is to deliver an assumption. Dan Mall, art director and designer, puts it this way:

"By default, presenting a full comp says to your client, 'This is how everyone will see your site." In our multidevice world, we're quickly moving towards, "This is how some people will see your site,' but we're not doing a great job of communicating that.**"**

—DAN MALL, "The Post-PSD Era" (*http://danielmall.com/articles/ the-post-psd-era/*)

It's hard to fathom any single browser rendering a design *exactly* like Photoshop does. Type differs based on the operating system and the browser, colors may shift depending on the screen, and then there are pixel density and resolution to consider. How bold is it, then, for designers to tell their clients, "This is how *everyone* will see your site"? Or how about trying to explain, "This is how some will see the site, and for some others it will be slightly narrower but not narrow enough for the navigation to break, but just imagine the tabs changing format and the footer becoming stacked vertically. *Are you following me, client?*"

The fact of the matter is, faulty communication is just one of the pain points full-page comps present—one of many, unfortunately.

Pain Point du Jour

Even the most unseasoned designer can attest to the parade of frustrations with every use of Photoshop. To be fair, there's an important distinction to be made yet again. The struggles we have with the process aren't necessarily the tool's fault, though there are a few we can accuse Photoshop of to be certain.

Whether you're running into these daily or every so often, you can find the following pain points on every "anti-Photoshop for RWD" manifesto.

Fixed-Width Comps

No doubt, this is the most obvious barrier to using Photoshop in an RWD workflow. The challenge becomes, "How do I generate enough fixed-width, static comps to convey a fluid layout?" The answer, quite simply, is, "You can't."

Let's break down why designing multiple fixed-width comps isn't the most efficient or accurate idea.

Three-Breakpoint Trap

A popular approach, and one I used to subscribe to, was that in order to suggest a responsive layout, I needed to make three versions of each page I was designing. I needed one at 960px for desktops, one at 768px for tablets, and one at 320px for smartphones. Sound familiar? Somehow, someway, those breakpoints were accepted as ironclad standards. Come to think of it, we know the reason: Apple.

The 960px width related to a 1024px desktop with some padding on the left and right, the 768px aligned with the original iPad in portrait mode, and 320px was the pixel width of the original iPhone (also in portrait mode). Though it has a considerable market share, Apple isn't the only game in town when it comes to devices. If our goal is to design for inclusivity, embracing the diversity of screens our sites will be viewed on, it's hard to justify these breakpoints being the only ones that matter.

Now, you might counter that notion with, "All smartphones will generally be around that size." Not only are we seeing smartphones that are much larger than 320px wide, but I think we do our designs a disservice by dictating adaptation only at predetermined breakpoints. Personally, I prefer to add breakpoints where the design is becoming stressed. **Figure 2.4** shows an example of main navigation at 960px wide3

Figure 2.4 Plenty of room for everything

As the browser gets smaller, there's still plenty of room for the navigation to appear. In fact, it could fit at 768px just fine (see **Figure 2.5**).

Figure 2.5 Less room but still adequate

It truly gets stressed only at 657px (see **Figure 2.6**).

Figure 2.6 *Now it's time to add a breakpoint.*

At that point, I think it's appropriate to add a breakpoint so we can tuck the navigation behind a trigger to expose it off-canvas. Would it have been the worst thing to add it back at 768px? Maybe not, but we'd be penalizing anyone with a device width between 680px and 767px by hiding the navigation when we didn't have to do that. To that point, the navigation might be the only thing changing at the 680px breakpoint because it happens to be the only one under stress, so why change every nonstressed element then? Hence, we employ as many breakpoints as we need based on how individual elements react to the screen width.

Why is this important? If we're using predetermined breakpoints to design comps, we're not allowing the design to adjust when it *needs* it. In Photoshop, it's awfully hard to know at what point design elements will get stressed in the browser and require change.

The Fallibility of Assuming 960px = Desktop

When we present a fixed-width, 960px comp, we usually introduce it as "Here's what the site will look like on a desktop." I've rarely, if ever, introduced it as "Here's what the site will look like on an iPad in landscape orientation," but that's just as accurate. It's only at this realization that I want to hustle back into Photoshop to make sure all the links are of "tappable" size.

It's inaccurate to make assumptions about the input of a device we're designing for solely based on the dimensions we gave the comp to begin with. Assuming screen widths are synonymous with specific devices can inadvertently set our focus on designing for "touch" at smaller widths or "clicks" at larger ones.

I was recently given a Microsoft Surface Pro 3, a device that presents itself as a tablet but is capable of running Windows 8. It's not difficult to switch between apps clearly geared toward touch interaction and traditional desktop apps that require a stylus and physical keyboard. Its 12" screen is comparable to most laptops, but its form factor aligns with tablets. With a resolution of 2160×1440, the Surface should be classified as a desktop screen, though that would be telling only half of the story.

How does that impact your 960px PSDs?

All the Comps!

The number of full-page comps can have a considerable impact on a project's timeline. The more you wish to show prior to development, the longer you delay moving to an environment where your design can be tested. Project time needs to be spent wisely.

For example, a client of mine wanted to know exactly how long the design process would take before I could start developing. I came to the conclusion that I'd need 20 page comps to feel comfortable moving ahead with code, and that it would take over two months to design them. The client scoffed until I spelled out exactly how many templates and screen widths needed to be considered.

It's easy to get bogged down making edits to comps, round after round. Even so, making a static representation of each page at each size does not guarantee the design won't break somewhere. The complexities of a responsive website build demand that you spend more time testing than you did on your fixed-width sites.

A folder's worth of page comps is also problematic to maintain. Having to make navigation edits across 20 comps is less than desirable. Being aware of the production effort is a good place to start. It's worth your while to look at the number of comps you typically produce just to present one stylistic direction (see **Figure 2.7**).

Figure 2.7 Is it me or is that a lot of comps? This still may be only a fraction of the comps created for some projects.

TIP If you're trying to maintain shared content across multiple PSDs, Photoshop CC can help. With External Smart Objects, any changes you make will be reflected in any PSDs that reference them. While it won't help with any width-specific layout alterations you need to make, it's useful for things such as color and text changes.

Whatever final number of comps you arrived at, imagine if we had to create three different directions for each. See my point?

The sheer effort involved with making fixed-width, full-page comps is significant in terms of time and money and potentially your sanity. Don't forget to make some comps of what these pages will look like on the CEO's "phablet!"

Lack of Interactivity

Static comps are, well, static. Without the help of the browser, there's no interacting with flat elements. The client asks, "What does that button do?" You reply, "It goes to the product detail page," as you shuffle through files to find product-detail.jpg. There are some ways around this that we'll explore in Chapter 10, but for now we're still stuck designing for an interactive medium via noninteractive deliverables.

> ❝It's time to stop making pictures of websites and start designing all aspects of the user experience simultaneously and in a practical way.❞
>
> —STEPHEN HAY (*Responsive Design Workflow*)

States

A considerable layer of design is lost when you can't show hover, active, and focus states in proper context. Often, we make extra JPEGs, turning on and off layer comps to achieve the right series of "states." Like everything else, the task becomes more complex the more screens we start designing for. It's simply not natural nor is it practical to expect to be able to account for every behavior and interaction statically (see **Figure 2.8**). We *should* be able to convey basic state changes without needing to string together multiple files. We're asking our clients to suspend reality and embrace the façade of the static instead of immersing them in the interactive.

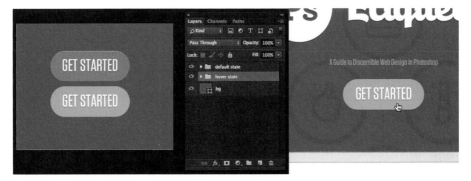

Figure 2.8 Photoshop (left) takes twice the assets, and effort, to pull off a simple hover done once in the browser (right).

Movement

Interactivity isn't relegated to rollovers either. CSS3 and JavaScript give us the tools to transition, transform, and animate to enhance interaction. I'd argue that these facets have become just as much part of "design" as colors and type. They contribute to the feel of a site in ways that other content can't. To put them off until the development phase seems to be leaving a lot on the table.

Every motion needn't be figured out at the infancy of a project, but the earlier you can introduce movement conceptually, the better. Here's an example: "You see this section? It's going to gracefully fade in from the right when you scroll down to it, calling attention to itself." Being able to show an idea like that might deter a request to make the hypothetical section bigger or bolder so it stands out on its own. Even the crudest of HTML prototypes can do a great job here.

I'm just not sold on the idea that we can convey movement well in Photoshop comps.

Fixed Positioning

Web designers—myself included—often abuse it, but I freely admit that I love using "background-position: fixed." Why? It's an easily executed technique that can add a great deal of depth. Typically it's used on large, "hero" background images, but the effect is unmistakable: The content above and below it scrolls by while the background stays anchored to the browser. It's a great method for layering sections and introducing some depth without necessarily needing shadows. The problem is, it's nearly impossible to suggest in a static comp.

For that matter, fixed positioning of nonbackground elements also falls along the lines of scrolling interactivity that can be produced only in the browser. It can be mocked up to an extent, but again, it's nearly impossible to communicate the feel it brings to a page. More importantly, fixed navigation can provide increased utility to the user, another benefit that can get lost in translation when presenting a static JPEG.

Some Fonts Are Better Than No Fonts?

The rise in support, and popularity, of web fonts in the browser has been one of the most welcome features for designers in recent years. With that came an interesting paradigm shift. We went from having all the permissible "web-safe" fonts on our desktop to a countless number stored online. Subscription services have libraries of thousands, yet because of licensing, it's not feasible to have them all available in apps like

Photoshop. It's kind of a bummer knowing what font you want to use and being able to use it in the browser but not while you're designing a comp.

The good news for Photoshop CC users is that it integrates the popular web font service Adobe Typekit. This is huge because experimenting with fonts is essential to the practice of creating full-page comps.

How to Connect Typekit to Photoshop CC

To access Adobe Typekit in Photoshop CC, follow these steps:

1. Make sure you've updated to the latest version of Photoshop CC.

2. Browse the fonts you want to have access to on *http://typekit.com*. Start by filtering fonts by Desktop Use in the right sidebar.

3. Choose a font and then select Use Fonts on the detail page. You'll get a dialog prompting you to launch the Creative Cloud app. Do so.

4. You'll be redirected to the Creative Cloud app, where you can see a list of all the fonts you've chosen to sync to your desktop.

5. Head back to Photoshop and find your chosen Typekit fonts in your fonts list. There's even a nifty filter to show only synced Typekit fonts.

The problem remains that not every font available to you on Typekit is licensed to sync on your desktop. If you use a different service, like Cloud.typography from Hoefler & Co. (*www.typography.com/cloud*), you can't use their fonts anywhere but the browser, unless you happen to own a desktop license as well. Font foundries and subscription services have made huge leaps to help Photoshop users experiment with fonts. However, because of licensing conflicts, all the fonts we can get in the browser aren't available to us on the desktop.

Rendering

Another common pain point when working with type is how it renders. Historically, type set in Photoshop looks different from how it looks in a browser. What's worse, if you're working on a Mac, there's no easy way to preview what type might look like in a Windows browser such as Internet Explorer. Why is that important? Have you ever completed the majority of front-end development, curiously checked how things looked in IE7, and realized that the font you chose was chunky and barely legible? The further you go in the process with a font, the harder it is to make a hard pivot and go with a substitute.

Photoshop CC users do have one nifty option of helping preview system rendering. In the lower right of the Character panel, you'll find the usual anti-aliasing options. Sharp is usually selected by default, though you may have opted for Smooth at some point. You should see a new option called Mac LCD, which will mimic how the system renders fonts. I've found it to be comparable to WebKit browsers such as Safari and Chrome. Again, the only problem is the lack of diversity: There's no setting close to what Firefox tends to do (it seems to make everything a bit bolder than other browsers) or any Windows options.

The Big Reveal

You've just completed the wireframes. Now it's time to turn those puppies into pixel-perfect comps. Excitement abounds as you take the next month to nail every detail of every page. Then again, given that you should probably show three different options for each, you might want to allow two months. Either way, this is what being a designer is all about: putting your head down and getting creative!

Then the time to present arrives. Butterflies. *Will they love it? I hope they don't pick Option 3 since we rushed that one last week just so we'd have three to show.* "OK, client, what do you think?"

"Let's go with Option 3. I like blue!"

Our tendency is to blame our clients at this point for having poor judgment. Sure, you poured your heart into Option 1 and slaved over the color palette for Option 2. But the last thing they saw two months ago was a gray box wireframe, and now they have these incredibly detailed comps to peruse. Their initial responses might seem a bit scattershot: "Where'd the phone number go? Cool carousel! Looks like they misspelled Johnson's alma mater. Hey, look, my favorite shade of blue!"

Full-page comps typically present our clients with a ton to digest. Content, style, and layout are all being assessed while we're just hoping they don't pick Option 3. The notion that we designers go behind the curtain and work our "magic" to blow everyone away with these comps is what's referred to as the *big reveal*. We bombard our clients with meticulously detailed mock-ups with no natural transition from a wireframe void of fidelity. Often the result is an overwhelmed client choosing what looks the most favorable to them: complete subjectivity.

> **"**Photoshop puts the focus on production, not productivity. Photoshop is about building something to look at, not about building something you can use.**"**

—JASON FRIED (*www.signalvnoise.com/posts/1061-why-we-skip-photoshop*)

You've also just spent months producing two other directions that were shot down. That's yet another blow to the efficiency you were seeking.

What Did You Expect?

When we set out to make full-page comps, what we aim to communicate is expectation: *This is what the home page will look like. This is what the fonts will look like. This is what the site will look like on a phone.* I hope I've illustrated some reasons earlier in the chapter why these aren't the most accurate statements you can make, but there's one more point to be made on the topic.

We simply can't deliver on the promise that a representation of a site done in Photoshop will render the same way in every browser. There are too many quirks to level the playing field. The easiest example is the difference between modern browsers that support CSS3 and older ones that don't. Whenever we use a fallback method to achieve an effect in an old version of Internet Explorer, how can we guarantee it will look exactly like our PSD? How meticulous would we need to be to make sure every element has the same amount of margin and padding in Chrome that it does in IE6?

Presentation Woes

How do you typically present your design concepts? Do you email your client a ZIP file? Do you pull up JPEGs and share your screen or project on a monitor? What assurances do you have that your design is viewed at 100 percent and not zoomed in or out?

For the longest time, I would place my comps in an empty HTML page and hack together some background repeater to give the impression you were looking at a real site. You see, the browser was a natural fit because it not only ensured viewing at 100 percent but seemed like the appropriate habitat for a website comp. It worked pretty well until I needed to show narrower comps at different breakpoints. The song and dance behind pulling up specific links on specific devices just to show a comp was pretty silly and *felt* like more work than it was worth.

Once, I had a client print out all the JPEGs I sent so they could make notes on them (see **Figure 2.9**). OK, maybe that's more like every time except once. It's almost as if they don't believe what I'm showing them is a real website, no matter how many disclaimers I throw at them: *Obviously you can't click anything but.... The background will continue to the full width of the browser if you can imagine it.... It's hard to tell now, but the navigation will stick to the top of the page as you scroll down....*

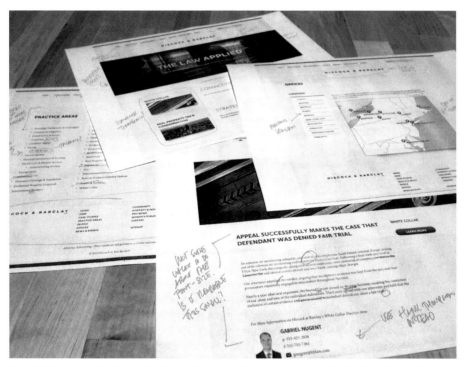

Figure 2.9 Truly an artifact from print design. There are better, more environmentally friendly options out there.

There's clearly something missing here in terms of presentation. The goal should definitely be to show our designs in the environment in which they'll live, but at what point do we just relent and develop the darn thing?

One of the major advantages to designing in the browser is the ability to make live changes on the fly. Want to try the buttons in red? It's the difference between editing a few lines of CSS (or one in Sass) and choosing every button on the comp one by one, editing the color, and exporting. With code, the change is reflected everywhere it's referenced. Many a designer has flipped many a table having to change a color or piece of text across ten different PSDs. Even if it's not for the purpose of showing a client during a presentation, this kind of off-the-cuff editing is beneficial for internal critique and ideation.

TIP There's no shortage of tools to annotate design in the browser, and RedPen (*www.redpen.io*) is currently my favorite. Simply upload your comp to the site, and it produces a link you can share with your team or client. You can even receive email alerts when someone has contributed a comment.

Bound by Approval

How do you assess whether a design is good? If design is how it works, we can't properly assess it without building it (see **Figure 2.10**). We could hack our way to suggesting functionality through a series of mock-ups, but not only would we continue to pile on the heap of comps we're making, we wouldn't get genuine interaction. *How smooth is the drop-down when triggered? Do the in-page search results load quickly? Will the parallax be off when I scroll?* (It will, by the way.)

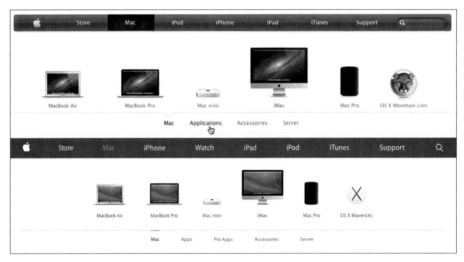

Figure 2.10 Good design takes details such as transitions and animation into account. For example, when Apple updated its website, it updated the animation of the product bar to be more subtle, matching the tone of the UI. That's hard to show in Photoshop.

The trap we often fall into is waiting until a client signs off on a comp only to notice in development that something significant needs to change. Sometimes it's because of a lack of communication with those developing our designs, but it can just as easily be something nobody saw coming until you start to test it in a browser. For me recently it was designing some spiffy circular avatars for employee profiles. Everyone seemed to love the style, easily achieved with border-radius and some box-shadow settings. But it wasn't until much later when we realized the portraits to be used weren't square like in my example but all different heights and widths. We could get close but eventually ruled in favor of nixing the circle approach.

Good design is tested and vetted. It's incredibly difficult to prescribe a solution without any assurances that it will hold up in the medium it's destined for. Approved static mock-ups typically don't allow the flexibility to explore design alternatives when you hit a snag in the development process. Rest assured, you *always* hit a snag in the development process. If you're looking for an example, consider those times when you didn't use the worst-case-scenario text length in your comp only for it to break the container in development.

Not So Stable

If I had a nickel for every time someone tweeted a complaint about Photoshop crashing....

Don't get me wrong—complaining about a Photoshop crash is a rite of passage for web designers, and deservedly so. Forget to save? Attempting Save for Web? Any time you see that pinwheel of death pop up, odds are it's all over but the crying. While I've personally seen fewer instances of Photoshop randomly crashing on me since upgrading to CC, there's no guarantee it won't happen at a crucial time. Does that mean you should stop trusting Photoshop? Perhaps, or maybe it means you should develop a swift Cmd-S (Mac OS)/Ctrl-S (Windows) reflex every 30 seconds just in case.

One of the main culprits of performance trouble derives from the fact that Photoshop gives web designers considerably more options and features than we would ever need. Liquify filters? 3D options? I can't recall ever needing them to design a footer. The weight of the interface options within Photoshop make slimmer, web design–focused apps attractive by comparison, no doubt.

Computer running slow? Isn't our first reflex to quit Photoshop? Granted, it's a powerful tool, but, boy, does it take up the lion's share of system resources to run.

Less-Than-Seamless Exporting

If there's one aspect of Photoshop that causes more headaches than the others, it's "How do I get this stuff out of my PSD?" The option Save for Web is historically the best bet, but it requires some prep such as cropping or slicing. Even when everything is ready, the patented Photoshop Color Shift option drives many of us off the deep end. You know the one: In your PSD it looks blue, but in your exported PNG it's green (see **Figure 2.11**).

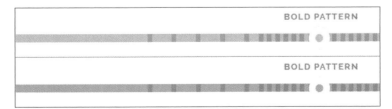

Figure 2.11 I've seen 30 solutions to the classic color-shift problem, yet none of them seems to work reliably.

In recent years, I've tried to circumvent the Save for Web process by using CSS3 to implement shadows, rounded corners, and more. Unfortunately, rare is the case that I can design a website without ever having to export a background image at the least. It's inevitable that asset creation will likely remain reason enough for keeping Photoshop in the fold, but that doesn't mean exporting is quick and easy (see **Figure 2.12**).

Figure 2.12 To say that slicing isn't the most efficient use of your time is an understatement.

Thankfully, in Photoshop CC Adobe introduced Generator, an extension that makes exporting assets from a PSD easy-peasy. If you're not familiar with Generator, there's a lot it can do, so much so that I'll spend a good chunk of Chapter 10 demonstrating it.

Empty Your Pockets

The cost of Photoshop is not insignificant. In fact, prior to Creative Cloud, a new copy of Photoshop cost about $700 if you couldn't upgrade or cash in on an educational discount. Compare that to tools like Sketch ($79.99), Pixelmator ($29.99), or Gimp (free), and it's apparent why the competition is attractive.

Easing the sticker shock, Creative Cloud not only provides Photoshop for a manageable monthly fee ranging from $10 to $50 but also gives you access to the entire suite of Adobe apps. Granted, if all you use is Photoshop, it will only take a little over a year to hit that $700 mark again.

Double the Effort, Double the Pain

One of the more hotly debated pain points of the PSD-to-HTML process is that you're essentially doing the same work twice. By making a static representation of a website, you'll inevitably be reproducing it in code. Why not start there in the first place?

For those on the pro-PSD side of the fence, the counterargument is that code is a bit abstract to manifest design. The ability to easily draw elements and shift their position and appearance without consequence isn't just a luxury but a necessity. Furthermore, those in the "pixel-perfect" camp prefer honing in on design decisions prior to code, as you'd expect.

While some would say, "Let's keep it rough and clean it up in the browser," pixel perfectionists would suggest that Photoshop is the better environment for evaluating and executing detail. In the former scenario, the refining depends on good designer/developer communication, whereas the latter continues to put design in a silo. Either way, establishing a picture to be re-created in code requires an additional amount of effort.

I stand firm against full-page comps. There are too many tasks I can create in the browser just as easily as Photoshop to make the extra time investment worthwhile.

If Not Photoshop, What?

In a search to ease the pain of a Photoshop-centric process, some have tried using other design apps, abandoning design apps altogether, or ingesting a large amount of aspirin. The most important thing is to realize when your workflow isn't making sense and seek adjustments and alternatives. Too often I talk to friends who acknowledge the conflicts I've described but relegate themselves to accepting them.

If you agree that producing full-page comps is problematic in an RWD workflow, you're clearly not alone. However, all too often the blame is placed on the software when it should fall squarely on the technique. That's like bashing in nails with a hammer and then blaming the hammer for not extracting them. All it takes is using the hammer differently to extract the nails, silly goose.

If you use Sketch, Pixelmator, Fireworks, or Microsoft Paint instead of Photoshop, I think that's fantastic. However, if you use those programs to create full-page comps, you'll run into the same problems. No matter how efficiently you can create them, static mock-ups still suffer the ills outlined in this chapter. In this, though, we find a new hope for the continued use of Photoshop in an RWD workflow, so long as we pledge to walk away from these detailed comps.

The anti-Photoshop brigade has little to stand on outside of preference. The people against full-page comps? Tons. That's why we need an alternative to the technique, not the tool.

All those voices clamoring for designing in the browser might be onto something.

3

THE CASE FOR DESIGNING
IN THE BROWSER

Have no fear—the subject of this book has not changed since you turned to this page, contrary to what the title of this chapter might suggest. We're still on track to design responsively with Photoshop. But a major component of a strong workflow is circumventing the painful full-page comp routine we just explored in Chapter 2.

There are a few options for doing this, though it seems we're all trying to find the single magic bullet that will solve all our responsive problems lately.

You Get a Tool! And You Get a Tool! Everyone Gets a Tool!

Wait! Can't we just throw more tools at the problem? Sure we can. When it comes to RWD apps, there are plenty to choose from, but three of the strongest are Macaw, Adobe Edge Reflow, and Webflow (see **Figure 3.1** on the next page). I highly encourage you to check out all three of them for yourself. Equally suitable is blindly subscribing to the following assessment.

Amid tons of revolutionary features, what makes these tools different from the Photoshops, Sketches, and Fireworks of the world is a fluid canvas. Imagine being able to resize a Photoshop document by dragging the corner of the canvas and seeing the contents respond. Picture yourself adding breakpoints to a comp so you can adjust presentation. Wouldn't it be great if Photoshop exported HTML & CSS? It does all of that and then some.

Figure 3.1 While RWD apps such as Macaw, Reflow, and Webflow offer great alternatives to full-page static comps, are they the only option? SOURCE: MACAW.COM, CREATIVE.ADOBE.COM, WEBFLOW.COM

There's really no catch here. Macaw, Reflow, and Webflow are all great manifestations of the wish list that web designers have had for years. Recently, I flirted with the prospect of making them a core piece of my RWD workflow, but ultimately I decided against it. Though all of these applications are completely capable of rendering the level of design I want, I found myself wanting total control, beyond the interface options. I want to write HTML & CSS just as much as I want to toy with layering backgrounds and tweaking type settings.

It's all about control. With so many moving parts, responsive design demands we take greater control of that which we can. There's so much we can't control: what screen someone pulls up our site on, the speed of the data connection they have, or the browser version they're using. What we can, and should, do is make sure our techniques are airtight. It's hard to trust anything except for code you've edited yourself to provide that level of granularity when it comes to realizing your design vision, regardless of the end user's platform.

Designing in the Browser 101

Truth be told, it took me a while to figure out what "designing in the browser" actually meant. I had the wacky idea that someone was actually drawing objects with

Photoshop-like tools in Firefox or something. Simply put, designing in the browser means exclusively using HTML & CSS to render design. The technique takes advantage of CSS's capabilities to render Photoshop essentially obsolete.

Photoshop Styles Translated to CSS

Here's a quick rundown of common Photoshop effects that can be achieved solely using CSS:

▶ **Transparency:** opacity: 0.5; color: rgba(255,255,255,0.5);

▶ **Drop shadows:** box-shadow: 10px 10px 10px #000; text-shadow: 10px 10px 10px #000;

▶ **Inner shadows:** box-shadow: inset 10px 10px 10px #000;

▶ **Rounded rectangles:** border-radius: 5px 0px 0px 5px;

▶ **Image borders:** border-image: url(border.png) 30 30 round;

▶ **Gradient backgrounds:** background: linear-gradient(red, blue); background: radial-gradient(red, blue);

▶ **Fonts:** @font-face {font-family: myFont; src: url(fontyfont.otf);}

▶ **Blend modes:** background-blend-mode: multiply; mix-blend-mode: multiply;

Note that, for blend modes, you can also use screen, overlay, darken, lighten, color-dodge, color-burn, hard-light, soft-light, difference, exclusion, hue, saturation, color, and luminosity.

Also note that this list omits browser prefixes that may or may not be necessary, based on ongoing browser support.

This is by no means a new method, though its popularity as an alternative to Photoshop has grown in recent years. At its foundation, designing in the browser is commonly done by editing code and previewing live or by altering generated code by inspecting elements in the browser.

Text Editor and Live Preview

It doesn't get more straightforward than this: Fire up your text editor of choice (mine is Coda by Panic, but others use Sublime Text, Dreamweaver, and so on), write some code, save it, and preview it in the browser of your choice (see **Figure 3.2** on the next page). See something you want to change? Head back to your text editor and change it. Refresh your browser. Look, Ma! I'm designing in the browser!

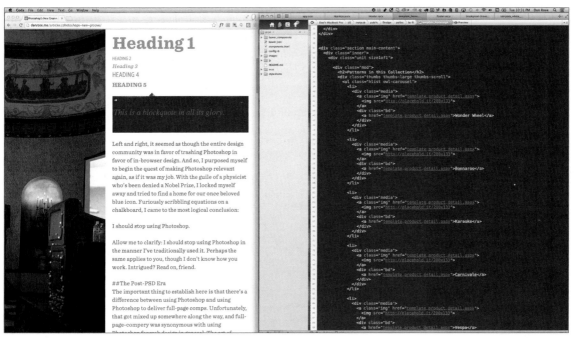

Figure 3.2 Depending on your workspace, editing code and live previewing could be a side-by-side view.

I imagine this do-si-do between your text editor and browser is familiar to most of you. There's no magic. The difference is that you're developing without the detailed script Photoshop comps provided. I'll get into the advantages of this method shortly, though it should be evident that cutting out the entire mock-up phase is a radical change from traditional workflows.

Not sure where to start "designing"? My best recommendation is to start with text—or, more specifically, all the "real" content. Assign each piece of text a tag corresponding to its hierarchical designation: <h1> for the page title, <p> for body copy, and so forth. Start playing with styles and layout from there. Sometimes it helps to take this approach and build your interface from the most fundamental element (type) outward.

"Content precedes design. Design in the absence of content is not design; it's decoration."

—JEFFREY ZELDMAN (*https://twitter.com/zeldman/statuses/804159148*)

Inspect Element

In addition to working out of a text editor, your browser's developer tools allow for real-time tweaks. If you're using Chrome, Firefox, or Safari, right-click the element in question and select Inspect Element (see **Figure 3.3**) to bring up the respective HTML & CSS (you can access the equivalent in Internet Explorer by pressing F12 or selecting F12 Tools under the gear icon). Being able to try something and immediately see the impact is a huge benefit and helps take the sting away from the experimentation we're used to in Photoshop (not completely, but it's a step in the right direction).

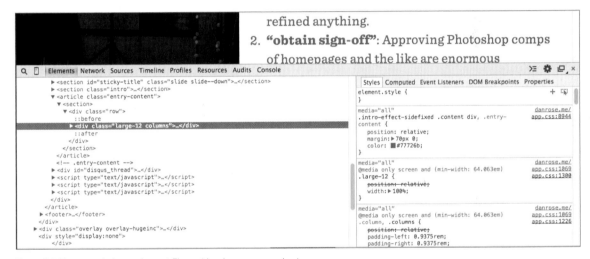

Figure 3.3 For many designers, Inspect Element has become second nature.

I've found it advantageous to stay within the developer tools and completely style an element before moving back to my text editor. At times, changing only a single setting in the browser makes sense, but often I prefer to establish a chunk of CSS (or HTML) I can copy and paste back into my production files. The key is to try to cut down on any inefficiencies in your workflow, such as switching back and forth between the editor and the browser with little payoff each time.

Fluid by Nature: The Inherent Benefits of the Browser

Fluid width in in-browser design means one thing: At last, we're freed from the shackles of fixed-width canvases. For me, there was this strange feeling when I first adopted the design-in-browser approach. I felt as though every block I put on the page was simultaneously more permanent and less permanent than when I did the same within

Photoshop. Although elements felt a bit more "published" because they were sitting on a web page, they also seemed to be hiding some hidden potential. Will it squish? Will it stack? Will it go away? I found the answer by simply resizing the browser, a valuable option missing from static design apps.

Do you find yourself going to a site and immediately grabbing the lower-right corner of your browser and then furiously pulling and pushing to see whether it's responsive? I feel as though this is an unspoken (probably even subconscious) behavior among designers. Whether it's a finished site or one you're just starting on, being able to resize your browser has become a natural behavior when evaluating design.

Speaking of evaluating design, just think of all the devices out there for a moment. We build device labs to try to get a good sense for how our sites render across the board, but inevitably we miss some screens of peculiar sizes owned by some of our audience. I've had some fairly significant layout issues to fix at uncommon devices widths such as 769px and 1025px.

Resizing the browser is the only way I would have found them before they reached the wild. Though it's not always 100 percent accurate, being able to adjust your browser to *every* screen width (and height!) goes a long way in thoroughly testing your design.

Interactivity

As I discussed in Chapter 2, Photoshop comes up incredibly short in terms of "showing" interactivity. I'd wager that this deficiency fuels the popular statement "Photoshop is not a web design tool." The Web is interactive, and designing for it shouldn't have to include faux-hovers and the like. We want the real thing.

Consider the case of toggling content. You might decide to use a convention such as revealing hidden text by pressing a trigger button. The markup is potentially similar, whether it takes the form of an accordion or otherwise. I find it much easier to experiment with ideas for interaction, including how fast the reveal appears, in the browser. Heck, it's nearly impossible to predict the speed at which something will animate in Photoshop. All the while, adjusting style for such content isn't all that difficult when the HTML doesn't need to change much.

Consequently, nailing aspects of interactivity and presenting them in the browser are fantastic for communication. No imagining required, except how the presentation might go with your clients. *Here's the hover state for submit buttons; give it a whirl. What do you think about that fixed background when you scroll? Check out the speed of the drawer that slides in from the right.* This is easily spoken to in the browser, but not so much (if at all) in Photoshop.

Global Changes

Have you ever taken on a project only to find out that something as crucial as the logo could be changing at any moment? *No worries! We'll just swap it in there when you're ready.* Sure you will. Given the client, you might also be signing up for changing the primary color or typeface of the UI at the same time.

If you're trying to make these kind of global edits in Photoshop, you have my sympathies. At least in CSS you can find and replace a specific hex value or easily change every instance of a font stack in one swoop. The mission becomes a cakewalk when you're using variables in Sass.

Photoshop simply isn't made for wholesale changes, no matter where or when in the design process they occur. Having to find every instance of a color, piece of text, or image across multiple PSDs is a nightmare. Conversely, when properly set up, code can be manipulated in a global fashion quite easily.

TIP While it doesn't let you make global color changes easily, Photoshop CC did port over the popular Character & Paragraph Styles functionality from InDesign. You can find these styles under the Window menu option.

True Font Rendering

I remember one of the first projects I ever got to use web fonts on. It was for a financial institution, and I couldn't wait to employ Calluna, one of my favorite serifs. It was one of those projects where you know the font you want to use even before getting to your computer. It was one of those even rarer projects where that first instinct ended up being the right choice in the end.

Well, almost.

Everything looked great to us, and the client was thrilled with Calluna in our Photoshop comps. So, we went ahead and developed it, sending them a first pass at a few templates. What they weren't thrilled about was how the Calluna font ended up looking in their browser of choice: Internet Explorer. Because we were going by the PSDs, we never caught how Calluna was borderline-illegible on any Windows browser because of the poor font rendering engine (it's gotten much better since, but credit that to the font foundry exljbris).

In fact, many web fonts still render poorly on Windows. Often, you'll find they look chunky and decrepit in contrast to their Mac counterparts. It's simply not something you can preview in Photoshop, but it can quickly temper your enthusiasm for your design as soon as you view it in the browser. The sooner you can test font rendering across browsers and platforms, the better (see **Figure 3.4** on the next page). Choosing an alternative at the beginning of the design process is infinitely better than after the client has gone from swoon to fury after development.

Figure 3.4 Though it can vary greatly between vendors, when it comes to font rendering, you know what you're getting when you design in the browser.   SOURCE: TYPEKIT.COM

Free

Contrary to what you may have been taught, you don't need Photoshop, or any design software, to build a web page. Every computer comes with a basic text editor and a browser at no additional cost. For some, it's the financial savings that make using text editors more desirable than purchasing Photoshop. Fire up TextEdit or Notepad and you're off to the races.

There are varying levels of what a designer might be willing to pay for a tool. You can certainly spend more for fancier text-editing apps, such as Sublime Text ($70) and Coda ($75), though there are free code editors such as Aptana Studio and Brackets. You're looking at potentially hundreds in savings compared to Photoshop, without the worry of incompatibility across versions.

1x the Effort

I recently gave the website Warby Parker a spin because my previous set of eyeglasses are covered with the typical battle wounds dads get playing with their toddlers. Besides offering the most hipster frames you'll find this side of the Mississippi, Warby Parker has a tool on its site that lets you upload a photo and preview how frames will look on you. Let's hear it for technology!

Seeing how the glasses will look on my face is nice and all, but I have no idea whether they'll press on the sides of my head, fall off my face when I look down, or pinch the bridge of my nose.

Figure 3.5 Warby Parker promotes its Home Try-On program as "5 Pairs, 5 Days, 100% Free." We're all attracted to quick, convenient, and painless shopping processes. Why shouldn't it be the same with design?

SOURCE: WARBYPARKER.COM

Thankfully, Warby Parker is best known for its "Home Try-On" program (see **Figure 3.5**), where the company will ship you five frames to try at your leisure. The preview tool on the site isn't worth the effort for me. I need to make my evaluation as "real" as possible.

That's how we should approach web design: one effort in the "realest" possible environment. Having to re-create a design in code seems incredibly inefficient, wouldn't you say? Designing in the browser ensures your efforts are applied to the final home of the design, as opposed to the temporary apartment that is Photoshop.

Perception plays a major role when deciding to abandon the Photoshop phase. While it's possible that specifying every last pixel in a comp will help give a developer a clear understanding of what to do, it also seems like an excessive effort compared to writing some code and iterating on it. The perceived amount of sheer design effort in Photoshop appears to be something we can circumvent by choosing to code instead.

❝HTML/CSS is real in a way Photoshop will never be.❞

—JASON FRIED (*https://signalvnoise.com/posts/1061-why-we-skip-photoshop*)

TIP As noted earlier, always use real content. I used to be a Lorem Ipsum-er back in the day. Using placeholder text is like shoving all your messy desktop files in new folder called Desktop Files. It's a temporary fix to a persisting problem. Eventually you're going to have to use accurate content, and the sooner you and your client can do it, the better.

How important is it to work toward something "real"? Wouldn't it seem like a bit of a waste to work on something that isn't part of the *actual* site you're designing? How can we defend it? In terms of potential time and money savings, eliminating any effort duplication is essential. This multidevice world demands that we work efficiently, and that means we need to lean on the browser much more than we have been.

Web Design's Natural Habitat

Clearly, we're seeing the stark contrast between a program designed to make pictures and an inherently interactive platform. For all these reasons and more, the browser is the best place to evaluate user interfaces and ultimately user experience.

The end goal of full-page mock-ups has always been completion: no detail left on the table and no pixel left unconsidered. The problem with this approach is that we do all of the evaluation within Photoshop, which lacks the credentials of fluidity and interactivity to make assessments properly. We never truly accounted for how the browser would impact the design decisions we've made. Better yet, we've never *embraced* said impact.

When we design in the browser, the checkpoints for evaluating user interface (UI) and user experience (UX) become more frequent, naturally. I always like to use site navigation as an example because of how many different forms it can take across screen widths. The moment you adjust your browser width, a horizontal navigation bar will either gain space or lose it. That's your first opportunity to change course, if necessary. The moment you switch to a different kind of browser from the one you're using, those same navigation items might render slightly more bold, therefore stressing dissimilarly to the previous browser. Again, it's an opportunity to adjust and move forward. Likewise, what happens when JavaScript is turned off and the menu doesn't have a signal to tuck underneath a trigger button?

If we can embrace designing for an innumerable number of screens, browsers, and sometimes settings, we can reach our audiences with accurately rendered design and without roadblocks. The only way of accounting for the diversity of the browser is to prototype directly in it. From there, we can test what works, why it works, and when it works.

If you come away with nothing else from this chapter, understand that the goal of a responsive process should be to ditch the concept of showing a single moment in time. For this purpose, the browser is superior to Photoshop because it encompasses every width, state, and behavior (moment) anyone could ever experience your design on. That's accuracy (see **Figure 3.6** on the next page).

Figure 3.6 If we're trying to be accurate, we'll have to account for all these devices and the ones coming out in the future as best we can.   SOURCE: COGNITION.HAPPYCOG.COM

Public Testing

A few years ago, I would have preferred to sing the National Anthem at the Super Bowl than show my clients in-progress Photoshop comps. In case you don't know me, you can assume that belting out "The Star-Spangled Banner" at the big game isn't exactly on my bucket list. I'm even skittish of showing in-progress Photoshop comps to the people I work with, never mind open myself up for critique and scrutiny on pixels that haven't been run through the layer style gauntlet yet.

Today, I prefer showing clients in-progress looks at design in the browser. *How's that accordion work for you? Any trouble filling out the form? Does the login sequence seem a bit over-designed?* While I can't put my finger on it, the browser appears to be more conducive to conversations about "how it works," which has just as much to do with design as "how it looks."

PSDs for Proofreading, Browser for Evaluating Behavior

Typically, edits to full-page comps are subjective, aren't they? Change this, change that, and so on. I'm not sure if your experience resembles mine, but the majority of client feedback on my comps was always, "Can you change the text to say _____?" All the while, I really wanted feedback on the effectiveness of interactive components. Photoshop comps almost always became a fancy exercise in proofreading.

The moment I shifted to using the browser for prototyping was the first time I started garnering the kind of feedback I truly sought. It was almost as if my clients finally understood, "It's in a browser, so he probably wants me to try using it." It was almost as if I finally understood how to show "design" to my clients. Too often, what gets lost in our comps is the function of design, buried beneath a sea of style choices. In the browser, the style choices still exist, but the window implores you to act.

Reaffirming Expectations That Things Look Different in Different Browsers

I've tried every disclaimer known to man in an effort to warn clients that what they're seeing in a static mock-up will look different in the browser. Even if everything rendered like a mirror image in Chrome, it's bound to look slightly different in Firefox and markedly different in Internet Explorer. It's not until you start prototyping in the browser that the inconsistencies between browsers truly become apparent to your client (see **Figure 3.7**).

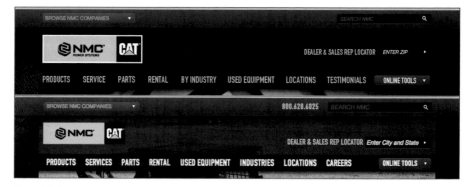

Figure 3.7 Font rendering, text positioning, subtle padding differences, and last-minute panic decisions such as adding the phone number make the PSD (top) different enough from the final site build (bottom) to reliably call the PSD an exact replica.

Why should we lead our clients to believe that the perfect comps we produce aren't attainable across browsers? Instead, let's expose our clients to the nitty-gritty differences of type, layout, and style from the outset in our designing. The earlier everyone can embrace these inherent differences, the better the opportunity for designers to deliver realistic expectations.

Easy to Change on the Fly

The ability to easily make global changes in the browser may open up better conversations with your team or clients. This may sound incredibly risky if you've always used traditional workflows, but I think you should try entertaining style changes *during* a meeting. Trust me, this will seem tame compared to some of the other tactics I recommend in this book.

The idea falls in line with showing in-progress design in the browser. Previously, we'd gear up for the big reveal and pull back the curtain of our pristine Photoshop comps. Let's scratch that completely. I'm not suggesting we rely on client input over our own design ability, but inviting our clients into the process of design has profound benefits. Not only do these in-progress conversations give us opportunities to educate our clients on many aspects of web design, but they also help stakeholders feel a sense of ownership without having to send you a list of 54 edits.

To pull this off, you need to be able to make changes on the fly. Presenting comps in Photoshop, we'd be clumsily exporting JPEGs and uploading them. I'm not certain how good your Photoshop ninjutsu is, but I know mine isn't at the level where I can pull off anything beyond a simple free transform, save, export, and upload while not skipping a beat in a meeting. Try making a change that swiftly to three different-sized comps or every other template you've mocked.

Editing on the fly in the browser typically produces results that will cascade where they need to, across widths and pages. From there you can have great discussions and quick critiques about what might work better without having to go back for a few days and set up another meeting.

All in all, the ability to test your design in the browser should only instill confidence that you're on the track of a usable, accurate design. We simply can't have the same kind of assurances in Photoshop without knowing how our designs will translate.

> **TIP** If your heart is set on designing on the fly in Photoshop, check out InVision (*http://invisionapp.com*). These brilliant folks have engineered a plug-in called Live Share, which allows you to make edits in Photoshop that will automatically update in your presentation.

Assessment as a Client Education Tool

If I'm not serving pizza or applesauce, my toddler almost always objects to what I present to her for dinner. Hey, she's two—give her a break. And give me a break for not being down for pizza every night.

Knowing the chances of culinary acceptance aren't high with her, I tried something different one time: I invited her to watch me cook. As she started making a connection between grilling chicken, steaming rice, and eating it soon thereafter, I could see her inclusion in the process was the missing ingredient, for lack of a better term. Yes, we need to include our clients in our design process, but that's not where this story is going. It's more fun than that.

You see, chicken is still pretty high on my daughter's yucky scale, so more had to be done to bring her around.

I started explaining *why* we eat certain things together (think: chicken and rice), as well as why we don't eat certain things together (think: ketchup and ice cream). In a very elementary way, I could see the explanation setting in. Knowing "why" is the primary component to every toddler musing. As adults, we sometimes forget to investigate the "why" and rely on our own biases and previous knowledge.

One of the hardest battles we designers fight is conveying all the design wisdom we have to design-averse clients. Some say educating clients on design isn't worth striving for, and it's true that we're hired to be the experts in our field and they in theirs. Still, we should do our best to inform our clients on objective issues rather than debate subjective ones with them.

Fold

The fold is my arch-nemesis—all the more so because of my ongoing struggle to convince my clients that it doesn't really apply to consuming content online. Traditionally, newspaper editors refer to the content on the top half of the front page as "above the fold." The goal was to feature the most important information above the horizon line to entice someone to pick up the paper and buy it. Repurposed for the Web, the idea is the same: Feature important homepage content in view without having to scroll.

With so many different device heights, browser toolbars, and personal preferences, it's impossible to target any pixel value as "the fold" to keep content above, since "the fold" falls at different places on different screens (see **Figure 3.8** on the next page). Furthermore, the argument is moot: Data supports the fact that users embrace scrolling and tend to get a good sense of what's on the page in its entirety anyway.

The previous reasons, told in much more detail, have become a key part of my shtick to clients. However, the conversation now comes up during early prototyping as opposed to previously when it was a topic for late development. Because I'm designing in the browser, it's natural for clients to ask questions about the fold before I even get into high fidelity. If you don't show static comps in the browser, this is a conversation you risk having at a very inconvenient time late in the process.

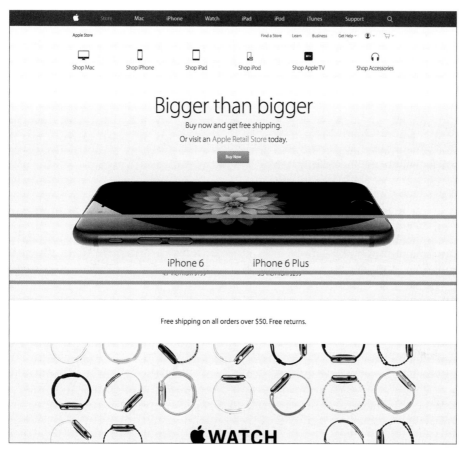

Figure 3.8 People have theorized this supposed "fold" is anywhere from 600px to 768px to 800px from the top of the page. Imagine if Apple decided to subscribe to pushing their WATCH content up to fit above 600px.

Explaining how browsers render type differently is best shown, ironically, in the browser. Conveying what's an acceptable "tap" size is far easier on a touch-enabled device than a comp on a desktop monitor. Evaluating the usefulness of animation, transition, and interaction is incredibly effective when you can show it. These client education aspects, and so many more, tend to be a natural part of the conversation when everyone is sitting in front of an actual browser instead of a picture of one.

Designer/Developer Bonding

While the historic rift between designers and developers may have been amplified only at the onset of responsive web design, the occasion also engendered a call for reconciliation. There's simply too much to consider between technology and technique to continue siloing both roles. Designers need a solid understanding of how browser behavior affects their work, and developers should be able to interpret a visual theme in all the overlooked nooks and crannies.

Much continues to be made about the blurred line between design and development. On the surface, a designer with some code chops and a developer with a discerning eye sound like ingredients for an unstoppable web pairing. Dig a little deeper, and you'll find that a shared vocabulary makes this scenario ideal. The conversations these folks have aren't happening in Photoshop on the command line.

They're happening in the browser.

Designing in the browser removes us from Photoshop, in the most literal sense. With HTML & CSS, we're operating on the same playing field as our developer counterparts (one of them, anyway) and can leverage their input to fully realize our design intent. We're using terms like *media queries*, *pseudoselectors*, and *progressive enhancement* in ways we most likely weren't in Photoshop. If you feel like Photoshop is your domain, and yours alone, try seeing how it feels to pair up with a developer and just start laying out a site beginning with code instead.

The browser harbors healthy designer-developer communication, and both parties need to contribute jointly and effectively to take on a myriad of moving (responsive) parts.

OK to Kill Photoshop Now?

No! Well, not entirely. As confusing as it might sound, we just need a better role for Photoshop in the aftermath of the design-in-browser movement. Clearly, we should be leveraging HTML & CSS as early as possible, but like Photoshop, code has its deficiencies too.

Those deficiencies provide the opportunity to keep Photoshop in the loop and transform our workflows into well-oiled machines. We may have killed the way we used Photoshop traditionally, but we won't be killing it altogether anytime soon. Hooray for happy endings!

This is where the fun begins: the romantic comedy that is Photoshop and the browser.

4

A PLEA FOR PHOTOSHOP– BROWSER HARMONY

In Chapter 3, I presented the case for a browser-based approach to web design. In this chapter, I'll take the browser approach down a peg, but I don't want to diminish its importance in a responsive workflow. The browser is still the centerpiece of what we're doing. But we need to work Photoshop back in to the fold—and not just because we're Photoshop fanboys and fangirls. If it didn't make sense to include Photoshop, I wouldn't waste your time advocating its importance in the responsive web design (RWD) workflow.

The good news is that Photoshop, more so than any other tool I can think of, fills an important role missing in a browser-only design process.

Photoshop Is the New Vinyl

Have you ever had someone send you a link to a YouTube video and, before you know it, you start going down a never-ending hole watching related video after related video? That happened to me recently, and it started with the popular show "How It's Made." My binge-watching led me to a fascinating piece on vinyl records. (If you just had to Google *vinyl records*, you're probably not the only one.)

The history of vinyl records is arguably more interesting than their manufacturing. Many of us remember their popularity in the 1970s and 1980s. Even when the cassette tape began to dominate music sales in the mid-1980s, records were still holding their own. It wasn't until the compact disc (CD) became the preferred music medium in the 1990s that vinyl records really fell out of favor. In fact, CDs were so superior to records for most music consumers' purposes that they pushed vinyl to the brink of extinction.

CDs offered a smaller, portable format that could fit significantly more music than records. They were even more durable, depending on how you stored them. It's no shock that CDs were became more popular than vinyl. When the iPod ushered in the digital music revolution of the mid-2000s and began to marginalize disc media, you would assume it made vinyl go away altogether, right?

Wrong. An incredibly strange thing happened: In 2006, people started buying more records. Today, vinyl growth is steady, and while it's by no means equal to digital in sales and mainstream consumer use, it remains relevant. Amazingly, market analysts have assigned no single concrete reason for vinyl's uptick in popularity (see **Figure 4.1**).

Figure 4.1 Vinyl has withstood some major innovations in music media, staying relevant even to the current day. Can Photoshop do the same in the face of new apps such as Sketch and workflow alternatives such as designing in the browser?

So, who or what gets the credit for sustaining the life of the vinyl record? Two main audiences: audiophiles, who prefer vinyl's sound quality and treasure their massive record collections, and disc jockeys (DJs). DJs have mastered the art of combining the digital and the analog, so to speak. Digital tracks play off a computer while the DJ spins a record on a turntable for scratching, looping, and adding a host of physical effects.

Curious, I sought after some rationale from a friend of mine who is a popular Boston-area DJ. Why does he prefer to use vinyl in his work? It's the same thing we Photoshop users enjoy but sometimes have trouble putting words to: direct manipulation.

The Power of Manipulation

At last, we find Photoshop's first legitimate way back into a respectable design process. It's unrealistic we'd completely abandon the visual techniques we've mastered for years in favor of code-abstracted design. One of the major reasons we tend to feel more "comfortable" in Photoshop is our ability to stretch, squish, shrink, and reposition elements. Sure, it's possible to do those things with CSS somewhat easily. However, those manipulations sit behind a wall of abstraction, adjusting values and refreshing to see the results (see **Figure 4.2**).

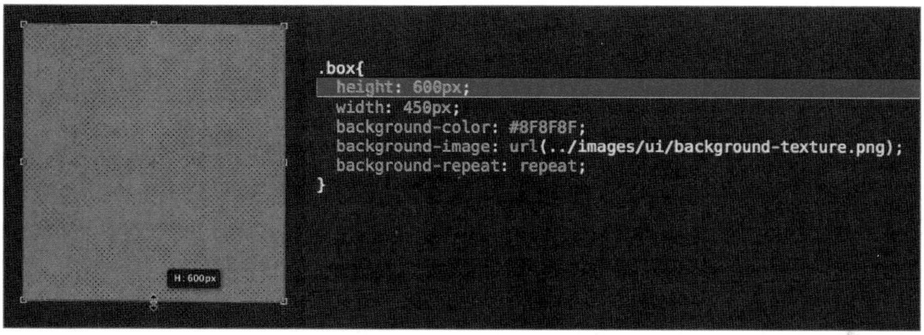

```
.box{
    height: 600px;
    width: 450px;
    background-color: #8F8F8F;
    background-image: url(../images/ui/background-texture.png);
    background-repeat: repeat;
}
```

H: 600px

Figure 4.2 The Free Transform tool, the Move tool, and a host of others offer an ease of use that enables the exploration we desperately need—and won't readily find in a coding-only design environment.

Designing in the browser can't compete with the benefits of direct manipulation. Don't underestimate the value of drawing a shape in Photoshop and seeing every step in its implementation. Your brain is processing all the sizes, colors, and positions, looking for the one that feels right.

> **"**I move shapes around until they make sense.**"**
>
> —JARED ERONDU (*https://twitter.com/erondu/status/465981370930450432*)

Sure, there are some disadvantages to the freedom direct manipulation provides. It engenders the "silo" effect, where we designers go solo and play in Photoshop for extended periods of time, discouraging collaboration. Direct manipulation is neither systematic nor object-oriented, meaning the process by which we transform type and shape often doesn't adhere to a pattern or set of preset constraints.

But exploring in Photoshop sure does help get the creative juices flowing.

Creative Mode vs. Correct Mode

I am usually superior creatively in Photoshop but better at being correct in HTML & CSS. I have a propensity to try outlandish ideas on the Photoshop canvas, knowing my actions have few repercussions, whereas when I'm coding, I'm sometimes fearful of not being able to revert to a point when everything was "working." Most designers I know operate this way, although a rare few are just as creative in code as they are in Photoshop.

As responsive web designers, we need to be "correct" in our execution of code, but we also need to be able to vet our ideas adequately. I'm just not sure we can do both in a single environment.

When I first set out to design in the browser, I assumed that because it had similar tools to Photoshop, I'd be able to explore creative ideas in the same way. I could not have been more wrong. Not only were my designs looking less distinctive and considered, but the amount of time I was spending on them increased significantly. I'd sit for hours in CSS just trying one thing, reverting, trying another approach, and never really nailing it.

This is where direct manipulation makes all the difference. Code abstracts design by a layer of syntax. Instead of choosing position, size, and color by dragging or stretching, we use letters and numbers to assign a value. By no means is the latter approach objectively wrong, but the former feels right for many of us. If you come from a print background, you most likely agree that this abstraction hinders your ability to ideate.

The more I've thought about this abstraction, the more I've been able to attribute it to one significant concern: following the path of least resistance.

The Path of Least Resistance

Even though we have the tools to pull off Photoshop-like effects in CSS, I don't think we always approach using them the same way.

Check out the audience navigation in **Figure 4.3** (on the next page). This low-fidelity prototype was built in HTML & CSS, and now it's ready for styling. My first impulse was to apply the button styles I was already toying with elsewhere and use them accordingly.

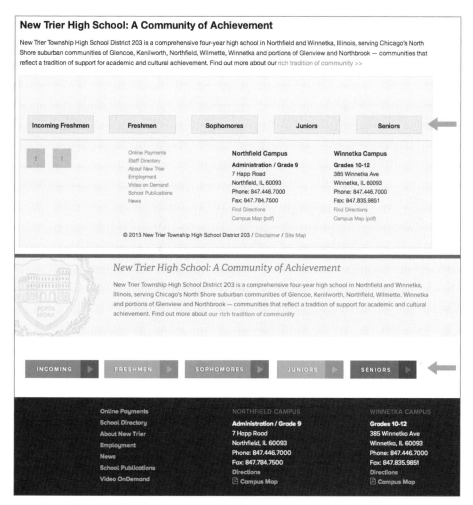

Figure 4.3 A styling-ready, low-fidelity prototype built in HTML & CSS

Objectively, there's nothing wrong with this approach, and certainly it communicates that these are five areas you can visit. When I showed the client, they were quite under-whelmed. The feedback I received was that the section didn't have adequate emphasis relative to the importance of the content.

My reaction was to fill the containing divs with the button color (see **Figure 4.4** on the next page). Bigger = more important, right?

Figure 4.4 Bigger buttons. Don't laugh—you would have done the same thing.

Again, the clients were underwhelmed. They expected to have buttons and appreciated the increased size, but they thought it was a missed opportunity to tell more of the story behind the content. It's a high school, and these portals are all part of the journey.

It wasn't until I toyed around with that section in Photoshop that I started to layer some new elements in, like screened photos and sideways text. The point isn't that those techniques are exclusive to Photoshop (because they're not: adding a simple background image and "transform: rotate" in an HTML & CSS editor is just as easy), but the idea came more naturally in Photoshop.

Sarah Parmenter had a similar assessment of designing in the browser.

> "It's a guilty secret I've been harboring for about a year: I cannot design directly into the browser. My creative brain switches at the point when I open my HTML/CSS editor (Espresso) and starts thinking in terms of structure and how to achieve the look of my design using as much native CSS as possible. If I don't have my design to follow, the whole process breaks down for me. I've tried, goodness knows I've tried, but my designs end up suffering, looking boxy, bland, and uninspiring."
>
> —SARAH PARMENTER (*www.sazzy.co.uk/2012/02/why-i-cant-design-in-the-browser/*)

Figure 4.5 A much more robust and considered direction

While I won't advocate for having your entire design predetermined before HTML & CSS, the example shown in **Figure 4.5** is a case where taking one small section or component into Photoshop makes a world of difference.

As unpopular as the idea may be, I think it's easier to take the path of least resistance in the browser than in Photoshop; working in an HTML & CSS editor makes you more inclined to think in terms of boxes, containers, and the styles you usually employ than ones you don't. Heavy layering, offsetting only a single element and not others, and breaking convention usually mean tweaking more than just a few HTML tags and CSS properties. Sometimes, that amount of trial isn't worth the inevitable error. Suffice it to say, for whatever reason, I'm more inclined to play it safe in the design techniques I use in code than in Photoshop.

Is it possible that lack of courage in our code-exclusive designs is the reason that all RWD sites look so similar?

Responsive Design Sameness

The idea that responsive sites all look the same isn't a new one. It's a topic that's been broached many times, and you'll find some interesting perspectives on it.

> "Have you ever noticed how many websites look the same? How many are just a bunch of rectangles? How many seem to copy from one another? Where's the uniqueness and creativity?"
>
> —STEVEN BRADLEY (The Web is a Rectangle, *www.vanseodesign.com/ web-design/rectangular-web/*)

> "I feel like responsive design has sucked the soul out of website design. Everything is boxes and grids. Where has the creativity gone?"
>
> —NOAH STOKES (*http://esbueno.noahstokes.com/post/44088237921/ where-has-all-the-soul-gone*)

> "I wonder if #RWD looks the way it does because so many projects aren't being run by designers but by front-end dev teams."
>
> —MARK BOULTON (*https://twitter.com/markboulton/status/ 445943150247702528*)

The question of "Why do all RWD sites look the same?" is a pertinent one when you consider that diversity in the pre-RWD era was fairly extraordinary. One could even argue that Flash-based sites were the most distinctive of the lot. Today, it's common-place to pick out the sites designed in the browser from ones designed in Photoshop et al. This notion is where we get such statements like "It looks like a Bootstrap/Foundation site" and "It's like they just slapped their logo on a responsive WordPress theme."

Figure 4.6 Examples of similarities in responsive site design. Common components include "boxy" layouts, white background headers, and hero images with white text overlaid.

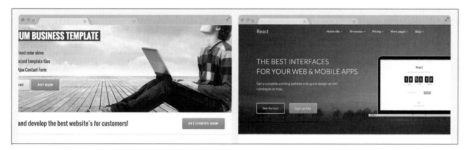

Figure 4.7 Examples of similarities in sites designed on the Bootstrap framework. Unadjusted button styles are a clear giveaway.

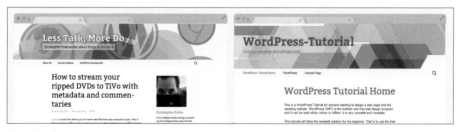

Figure 4.8 Examples of similarities in sites designed as WordPress themes. Similar content layout is a hallmark of blogs.

To some extent, there will undoubtedly be shared styles and components from site to site, no matter how original we think we're being (**Figures 4.6-4.8**). That's OK. I'd much rather have a Web that works than one that succeeds in diversity for diversity's sake. Remember, the originality we established using Photoshop didn't always translate to the browser in a way that was user-friendly, either. Karen McGrane made this witty retort to the complaint of RWD sameness as it applies to print:

"But why do all the magazines have the binding on the left? And columnar layouts, so tired. Where's the innovation?"

—KAREN MCGRANE (*https://twitter.com/karenmcgrane/status/515162632551411712*)

I'm not sure we can fault responsive design for a lack of uniqueness in sites, but certainly its introduction has added to the number of design considerations we need to make. By extension, new considerations may not always be tested across all screen sizes, so we rely on what "works" and what's familiar. We're still getting our feet wet designing responsively; creativity will come.

That doesn't mean we need to stifle uniqueness or "soul" in the name of being responsively correct. We need to think creatively about being creative.

"Emulation is a part of the evolution of design. And the web, for that matter. But design sameness tends to fade when one forgets all of the existing patterns, all of the Bootstraps, all of the preconceived design solutions. Design sameness fades when designers stop focusing on which solutions for their problem are out there and start focusing on the problem at hand."

—STEPHEN HAY (*www.the-haystack.com/2014/03/21/responsive-design-sameness/*)

I contend that Photoshop can greatly assist in our efforts to infuse our designs with the unconventional and unique. Where designing in the browser may introduce friction in the creative process, Photoshop can help us focus on the best approach regardless of the amount of code needed to execute it.

Using Photoshop Only When Necessary

Photoshop can ride along with designing in the browser, but we need to determine to what degree. It would be counterproductive to revert to full-page comps, but we still need Photoshop to throw down some high-fidelity ideas on. Likewise, we still need the browser to keep our designs flexible, while curtailing the amount of time and effort we exhaust trying to come up with truly unique ideas.

If a responsive workflow is your goal, I recommend adopting the following philosophy: *Photoshop can't be the workhorse we've made it in years past.* Instead, Photoshop takes a backseat to in-browser design, but we still use it to ideate when necessary. To what extent do we keep Photoshop involved?

In his article "Responsive Web Design in the Browser Part 1: Kill Photoshop," Josh Long makes the following statement:

> **"**If you want to be a better designer, I'd start by killing Photoshop**"**
>
> —JOSH LONG (*http://blog.teamtreehouse.com/responsive-web-design-in-the-browser-part-1-kill-photoshop*)

While some of this sentiment seems in line with what we've explored, I object to the notion that discarding any tool makes you a better designer. Becoming a better designer has more to do with knowing the limits of the tools you use and knowing when to use them for the greatest gain.

The browser can bear the majority of many layout and style decisions, which is great because it's ultimately where our design will live. We'd be shooting ourselves in the foot if we tried to make every decision before writing a line of HTML or CSS. That puts the onus on adopting a workflow that allows the flexibility needed to refine design solutions after being in the browser (I'll talk more about how to sell this kind of process internally and externally in Chapter 12).

The Megaman Principle

Raise your hand if you're also a child of the 1980s and grew up playing Nintendo. No, not you, Wii whiz kids. Not you, Atari fans. I'm talking about the 8-bit Nintendo Entertainment System. Specifically, I'm talking about my favorite series of games: Megaman.

For those unfamiliar, Megaman was pretty much the best thing ever. You controlled a blue, android-like robot in a classic quest of good versus evil. Your mission was to take down an army of bad robots, each of which had a unique weapon, be it ice, fire, stones, bubbles, or the even more obscure piles of trash Junk Man used. When you defeated these bad guys, you'd inherit their weapon.

In most instances, you'd be hard-pressed to find a use for your default Mega Buster arm cannon, so the quintessential strategy for beating each boss was to use another's weapon. Ice Man's Ice Slasher was critically effective against Fire Man, for example. Choosing the right weapon at the right time was, essentially, a glorified game of Rock-Paper-Scissors. Mastering when to use each weapon made the game infinitely easier (see **Figure 4.9**).

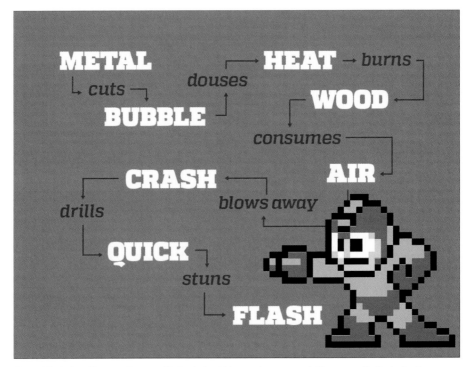

Figure 4.9 Just as Megaman leveraged timing to beat his enemies, can we do the same with Photoshop? Specifically, I mean the enemies called "boxy," "bland," and "uninspiring."

Collecting weapons and knowing when to use them is not so different from the problem we face in web design. By using the right tool, at the right time, for the right purpose, we extract more out of said tool than normal. Knowing when to use Photoshop is the only thing that can logically keep it in our workflows. Using it too often, too early, or for the wrong purpose produces frustration, wasted time, and potentially wasted money.

Practical Photoshopping: An Overview

In the next few chapters, you'll look at when, why, and how to use Photoshop alongside the browser. Because every project is different, implementations will vary, but you'll discover a few inventive ways of getting the most out of Photoshop.

Inspiration

If our plan is to present multiple design concepts to clients, where does RWD fit in? It seems like a daunting task to show contrasting design directions through Photoshop mock-ups at a few different sizes, so what's a more effective way to move the project forward?

The secret may be getting everyone on track toward a shared ideal far before anything is done in Photoshop. You'll explore a few ways to hedge what would otherwise be discarded work by using inspiration from around the Web to drive your directions. Equally important, you'll discover techniques for extracting more useful feedback from your clients.

Art Direction

The conundrum of page comps in a responsive world hasn't been ignored. While some of the industry has turned to producing tools to make comps more quickly, a strong contingent of designers have devised better design documents altogether. You'll take a look at this landscape in Chapter 6, including one I find to be the best suited for a responsive process: element collages.

Building Blocks

You may have created style guides in the past or be familiar with their longstanding print implementation. I'll define what style guides mean for the Web and, more importantly, as part of a responsive process.

Similarly, component (or pattern) libraries extend what's introduced in a style guide into functional collections of elements.

While it behooves us to develop both of these elements in code, there's plenty of opportunity to spice them up in Photoshop, long before we run into any funky page designs.

Repair

It's incredibly optimistic—naïve, even—to expect all the disparate elements of a responsive site design to come together seamlessly. When it's time to build pages from components, we usually find ourselves scrambling to make everything look like the coherent page it should be.

Let's determine to expect the wonkiness of putting components together and combat the seamless spots with Photoshop. You'll take a look at some common examples of where page design can fall short and feel disjointed in the absence of a system and pivot swiftly into an environment to try some stitch-work.

All of this preparation will lead to the union of Photoshop and the browser and to a better responsive workflow.

5

VETTING DIRECTION

Ordering takeout always provides great respite from having to cook another meal, so naturally it's an exciting event in my household. If you've ever been the one responsible for organizing the occasion, I'm sure you can relate to the following exchange:

Me: "What do you want to get for dinner?"

My wife: "I don't know."

Me: "How about pizza?"

My wife: "Eh. We just had pizza the other night."

Me: "Chinese?"

My wife: "We always get Chinese. I want something different."

Me: "Mexican?"

My wife: "…"

Me: "Barbecue?"

My wife: "…"

(long pause)

Me: "Pizza?"

The point I'm trying to make isn't that my wife is a picky eater because when the roles are reversed I find myself responding the same way. It's natural to want to know the options before committing to ordering takeout. Chances are there's something you can rule out immediately. Then there will be a few options you're just not sure about. Rarely will anything sound amazing, but eventually you'll settle on something that "feels right" at the moment. This is life.

The Contrast Conundrum

The best thing I can do as the organizer is to offer contrasting options. If pizza gets an unfavorable response, following up by naming 70 pasta dishes might be a frustrating way to find out she's not feeling like tomato sauce tonight. Suggesting Chinese starts to broaden the landscape of possibilities.

Your clients and stakeholders appreciate being presented with contrasting options, too. With so much to do in a responsive project, you need to be efficient in presenting options while also being aware that subjective views don't always make for the best designs, either. Up until now, I'm not sure that we, as designers, have always recognized that.

The Comp Approach

Traditionally, designers have shown options across three full-page Photoshop comps. The directive I always received prior to making three comps was to make sure each was noticeably different from the others. The elements could stay the same, but their styling needed to be unique (see **Figure 5.1**).

For the most part, getting a client to agree to one of three directions has a high success rate, at least in my experience. On the flip side, three flavors of comps is a bit more effort than most would prefer, only to eventually have two of them trashed. In recent years, I've noticed the rising popularity of presenting just one direction to mitigate this expected loss. The idea here is that you can will the design direction by starting with your recommendation and revising it based on client feedback.

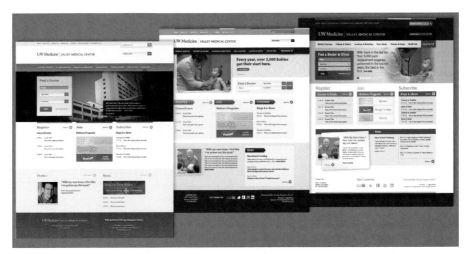

Figure 5.1 Option 1 (left) was always my favorite, Option 2 (middle) was acceptable, and Option 3 (right) the direction that took into account client requests. Much to my dismay, Option 3 always won.

I adopted a one-direction approach for a few years before noticing patterns in the feedback I was receiving. I was getting significantly more style prescriptions than I expected. *Can we change this to green? How about we add some depth in this background? Can you try seeing how it looks in a sans serif?* I began to feel offended. My reaction to was appease their requests with a "I'll show them how bad this looks" attitude.

They always liked seeing their suggestions. Go figure.

Within the Realm of Possibility

The root of the problem had little to do with establishing my design credibility over theirs. It's likely your clients will defer to your decisions, but they'll feel more confident when they can see the possibilities first. If you think about how this applies to style, it's all about presenting contrast.

Why was it so important to establish three unique directions in the first place? In doing so, you established contrast from one to the next, essentially showcasing the spectrum of possibilities worth critiquing.

You need to use contrast in order to properly vet style direction because without it, you have only one possible solution. Consequently, exploring multiple style directions helps keep you in check. Too often, designers put their heart behind a single approach too early in the design process, without giving due diligence to other viable solutions.

It may not be your preference (or mine, for that matter), but it's necessary to present contrasting style directions.

At the time I was debating the merits of presenting a singular style direction versus multiple approaches, my design director at WSOL, Dennis Kardys, had me watch a presentation given by Microsoft principal researcher Bill Buxton based on his book *Sketching User Experiences* (*https://vimeo.com/5189134*). Buxton puts this "exploration of alternatives" concept frankly.

> **"**When I come in with five [ideas] and I haven't made up my mind [about favoring one], guess what? I don't care. You can get rid of it; there are still four left.... If I come in with one idea and you criticize my idea, you're criticizing me.**"**

This comment was made in reference to the internal design process and thinking at Microsoft. The same can be apply to your own approval processes, including interactions with your clients. To be truly effective, you must have transparency in your design workflows, and that means involving your clients.

Including Your Stakeholders in the Design Process

The important lesson I've learned, and am still struggling to apply, is that it's disadvantageous to take away choice from your clients and stakeholders. That's because it's not so much about giving choice as it is about inclusion in the design process.

In my experience, clients appreciate taking a role in the design process that's more active than simple approval. I've yet to encounter a client who's requested that I show them less work or just fully polished work. Sharing your thought process and how you develop your ideas should help your clients understand the rationale behind a design more completely than a wireframe-to-comp process would.

This transparency does come with a critical shift away from the traditional roles you and your clients may be familiar with. They are allowed to partake in the inner workings of the design process, but they are not there to approve or disapprove of your individual design choices. Rather, your client's role is to supply more insight into their organization and industry and approve or disapprove the course you're on as you work through the design.

No longer can you view the role of the client as an annoying but necessary gatekeeper that you involve when it's convenient. With so many considerations in play when you're designing responsively, you need your stakeholders to be deeply involved and make sure you're on the right track. If you go too far before showing them anything, you've wasted valuable time and resources. You need your clients to be valuable contributors. As such, you're looking for a "keep going with this" instead of an "approved—make it so."

The primary difference between "keep going" and "approved" is expectation. The former suggests that what's shown isn't necessarily polished or complete, but its spirit is in line with where it needs to be. In other words, you have the green light to keep developing this direction. There may be some change down the road but not a significant departure from what you're showing. "Approved," by contrast, says, "You may proceed, but I'm expecting this to be the final execution."

Approval can be poisonous to a responsive workflow for many reasons. You need the browser to influence stylistic choices such as typography (think: rendering), layout complexities and breakpoints, and performance. Locking yourself into a certain to-the-pixel execution prior to front-end development is more likely to produce problems than solve them. You need a degree of flexibility in execution—not *carte blanche* to change anything at any time but a realistic expectation that your style will evolve the more you develop.

It's no wonder some designers are even being so transparent as to open their sketchbooks to clients.

> **"**Emphasize process. We are increasingly looking less for 'approval' and more for permission to move forward. Sketching provides visual evidence that we are iterating and evolving to solutions. It's easier to say 'okay' when no pixel is final. Sketches convey fast and temporary.**"**
>
> —JASON DZIAK, Happy Cog (*http://cognition.happycog.com/article/opening-my-sketchbook-to-a-client*)

Inviting your clients into your ideation should help curb the need for the *big reveal* and having to deliver a final comp before your clients can visualize this style. Instead, you and your clients can work toward the *big inclusion*.

On the road to the big inclusion, there are better deliverables to vet direction than full-page comps. Let's leave detailed design decisions for another day and instead focus on the bigger picture. Are there any directions not worth exploring? What competitor sites align to the same goals you have? What emotions do you want to evoke through the design? Answering these questions with a full-page comp is overkill.

Moodboards

Let's face it, at the beginning of a project, the spectrum of web design possibilities is so wide that you have no choice but to start narrowing your focus. It's often most practical and efficient to narrow focus by using examples from across the Web. If you can have constructive conversations about inspiration, you can hope to bypass a major problem of comping: assessing style and content simultaneously. It should be your goal to have separate conversations about style and content.

A great way to do this is by using *moodboards*. While the shape of a moodboard varies greatly, the goal is fairly common: to confirm that everyone is on the same page by hanging onto what has promise and chucking what doesn't.

Aten Design's Ken Woodworth explains the purpose of moodboards as follows:

> **"**What we really want to know, after the design kick-off call, is that we have a good understanding of the design direction the client is looking for. We talk a lot with clients about sites they like and how that applies to their project.**"**

> —KEN WOODWORTH (http://atendesigngroup.com/blog/mood-boards-evolution)

TIP Services such as Pinterest make great vehicles for collecting and presenting moodboards. Many inspiration-gathering apps have integrated some sort of sharing function that cuts down on the work of assembly and document creation.

Often, moodboards are collections of Internet ephemera. Borrowing from their print application, type, layout, and color inspiration are arranged on a "board." Each board can house one or more themes—or, in Aten's case, categories.

Methods of Moodboarding

The format a moodboard takes has everything to do with juxtaposition. Let's look at two extremes.

Traditional Collaging

Traditional collaging is the format most people think of when they hear "moodboard" (see **Figure 5.2**), likely because of its print application. The idea is to create an environment that conveys the aesthetic you're presenting. For example, one moodboard for a military organization's website might have conventional examples of stencil typography, an olive green and tan color palette, and action photography. Another board might contrast that direction with industrial typography, dark backgrounds and sharp accents, and studio portraiture.

Having been collaged together in Photoshop, the juxtaposition of these elements attempts to communicate the feel of a direction. It's common to name moodboards by characteristic, such as "Traditional Combat" or "Stoic Contemporary."

Organic Inspiration

A moodboard may not be so much a deliverable as a conversation. In an organic approach, designers and clients share what web aesthetics they find appropriate for the project, and several links are compiled to visit (see **Figure 5.3**).

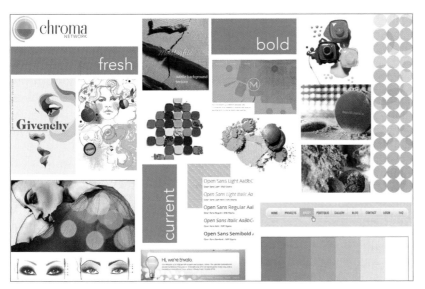

Figure 5.2 An example of a traditional moodboard with elements close to one another SOURCE: MAYA BRAGG

Figure 5.3 An example of documentation after a conversation about inspiration
SOURCE: ATEN DESIGN **GROUP**

A footwear manufacturer might share competitors' sites, while the designer might contribute contemporary examples of good design. This method should help establish a shared aesthetic, even though it's just a conversation at its infancy. For later reference, you may choose to create a structured document from your findings. Calling it a moodboard would be appropriate since what's captured is a collective "mood" to be explored.

In either method, the moodboard that's deemed most appropriate gives the designer an educated starting point for further exploring style, confident that the other directions may not yield the best results.

Finding and Storing Inspiration

If you're going to use moodboards, you'll need two essential ingredients: a reliable source of design inspiration and a way to document it.

There's no shortage of design inspiration galleries out there. You most likely already have a favorite or two, but if you're in the market for one, here's some advice for finding one.

It Has to Be Updated Weekly

Web design, style especially, seems to change daily. Rarely does a week go by without someone, somewhere launching a stellar website with a new approach. Keeping up with these contributions takes considerable time that most designers do not have. Therefore, make sure the site you choose to grab inspiration from is updated frequently so you're always on the front end of what's happening.

It Should Have Powerful Search Filters

Showing what's hot in web design is all well and good, but when you're looking for some inspiration for navigation, you'll have to manually sift through each one to find it. A good source of inspiration has filters such as categories or tags to help you find what you're looking for much easier. Blue, pink, header, footer, or whatever you're trying to find, you should be able to find it quickly.

It Should Have Multiple Channels of Communication

I usually like to start my day by visiting design inspiration blogs, but some days I just need to dive into project work or I can't find my way out of my inbox. If your favorite gallery doesn't have a way of nudging you every so often when site examples have been added, you may be missing out on some great inspiration. A Twitter account is typically sufficient, and sometimes an email newsletter is even better.

Here are some examples of excellent design gallery sites:

▶ Pattern Tap (*www.patterntap.com*; see **Figure 5.4**)

▶ Niice (*www.niice.co*)

▶ Media Queries (*www.mediaqueri.es*)

▶ Unmatched Style (*www.unmatchedstyle.com/gallery*)

▶ Site Inspire (*www.siteinspire.com*)

▶ Dribbble (*www.dribbble.com*)

Figure 5.4 Pattern Tap by ZURB (*www.patterntap.com*) has a thorough list of ways to filter your search.

If your go-to gallery should pack up shop tomorrow, would your moodboarding be in trouble? Just because a design blog filters its content doesn't mean you can't too. I highly recommend creating your own notebook from which to pull examples for moodboard use. Categorize entries similarly or completely different, but having a secondhand catalog of design inspiration can be super-helpful.

Here are some examples of cataloging tools:

▶ Evernote (*www.evernote.com*)

▶ Pinterest (*www.pinterest.com*)

▶ Ember (*www.realmacsoftware.com/ember*; see **Figure 5.5**)

▶ Kippt (*www.kippt.com*)

▶ Raindrop (*www.raindrop.io*)

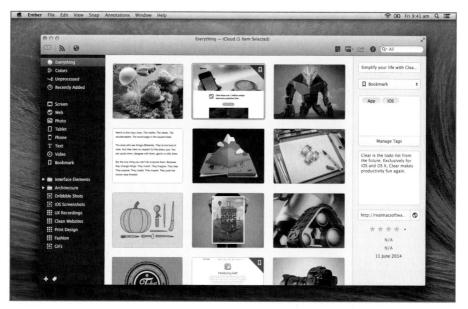

Figure 5.5 Using an app like Ember to save your inspiration is a great way to customize your archive.

Visual Inventories

Even before you jump into Photoshop or the browser, it's generally good to have a plan of attack. Contrary to what we might tell our clients, we don't "blue sky" great ideas, and they're never 100 percent original. That doesn't mean they're not valuable, but our ideas usually come from consuming what's currently appealing in our space. Simply put, we find what works well elsewhere, and that infuses our designs a little or a lot.

As you open up your design process, it's useful to work toward a shared understanding of what an appropriate design aesthetic is. Instead of attempting to defend flat design or slab serifs at the point of a mock-up reveal, why not have an open critique before it's applied to someone's brand? I structure these types of conversations around a document called a *visual inventory*, an idea introduced by Superfriendly's Dan Mall.

In the form of a PDF, Keynote, PowerPoint, or even a series of JPEGs crafted in Photoshop, a visual inventory is a presentation of existing conventions that comprises a conversation about art direction through the lens of industry-established approaches (see **Figure 5.6**). While it's certainly possible to email such a document, I highly recommend scheduling a meeting to present it instead. The purpose isn't to have everyone involved spend days scouring the Internet for the site they want to emulate most.

Rather, it's to receive input on which look, content, concept, and tone have significant enough value to pursue.

Figure 5.6 Visual inventories provide a good look at the current landscape of the Web, unearthing possibilities for your clients.

The primary difference between a moodboard and a visual inventory is format. Moodboards attempt to capture an environment or feel through collaging, while visual inventories home in on specific attributes individually and sequentially. The structure of the document is open to interpretation, but I usually roll with the following:

▶ Introduction (explaining the purpose of the exercise)

▶ Concept (vehicles for presenting story)

▶ Color (schemes and applications)

▶ Typography (specimens and combinations)

Defining Contrast

It's critical to lead your clients to give input that's in harmony with one direction over another. Otherwise, you'll get feedback similar to the following: "I guess that could work for us. We'll have to see it."

Here are some helpful ideas for presenting concepts high in contrast. Not everything will be pertinent to the project you're working on, but these are a good place to start.

Concept

- ▶ Linear storytelling (single-page scroll)
- ▶ Nonlinear storytelling (multipage exploration)
- ▶ Large photography
- ▶ Virtual tour
- ▶ Lifestyle video
- ▶ Human narrative
- ▶ Device-centric narrative
- ▶ Color scheme
- ▶ Bright and saturated
- ▶ Grayscale
- ▶ Light backgrounds

- ▶ Dark backgrounds
- ▶ Monochromatic
- ▶ One strong accent
- ▶ Device-centric narrative
- ▶ Typography
- ▶ Humanist serif
- ▶ Old-style serif
- ▶ Geometric sans serif
- ▶ Grotesque sans serif
- ▶ Handwritten
- ▶ Modern script
- ▶ Blocky slab

Within each section, try to find at least three different directions to explore. Pair each one with an existing site that executes the approach well. For example, under Color, you might show a light scheme, a dark scheme, and a saturated scheme. A convincing example of a light scheme might be Apple.com, whose iconic use of whitespace and gray tones exude openness and clarity but can also be read as more stark than friendly. Those characteristics are what you're looking for a client to align to, not subjective views on if they "like" Apple.com or not (see **Figure 5.7**).

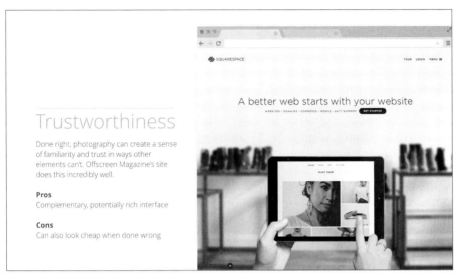

Trustworthiness

Done right, photography can create a sense of familiarity and trust in ways other elements can't. Offscreen Magazine's site does this incredibly well.

Pros
Complementary, potentially rich interface

Cons
Can also look cheap when done wrong

Figure 5.7 The template for a visual inventory is fairly open, but you'll want to include some commentary on an approach and an example from the Web at the least.

The Pursuit of Efficiency

Part of the problem with presenting three full-page comps is that it requires you to produce three different, fully fleshed-out designs. Alternatively, a visual inventory allows you to vet any unworthy directions without such effort. For example, I worked on a project where I presented three type directions: humanist serif, geometric sans, and handwritten. Going into the presentation, I really thought they'd favor the handwritten because it appeared to reflect the brand's whimsical nature. The client shot it down, informing me that they had used a handwritten font previously during a period when the company was publicly criticized. They felt that running with a handwritten font would harken back to a previously poor image and public perception.

If not for the visual inventory, I would have spent hours mocking up their site in handwritten type, only for it to get trashed (see **Figure 5.8**). I'm not suggesting that you shouldn't explore unfavorable examples in subsequent exercises. If you can make a case for further exploration, by all means, do so. Just be cautious of a strong reaction, especially if it's supported by objectivity, as was this example.

vintagehope.co.uk

Vintage Hope, a retail china gallery, takes a refined industry and bends it towards whimsy with its handwritten type.

In much smaller doses (think buttons or subheadings), handwritten type might be more approachable to students.

Figure 5.8 Designing this screen for a visual inventory took four minutes. A comp that used handwritten type across the UI would have taken hours.

Again, the objective of this exercise isn't for a client to approve a monochromatic, single-page scroll with slab serifs. Rather, the objective is to start a critical conversation about how different elements of the Web can best represent their brand. Could a bright color palette infuse the sense of activity your company is seeking? Might an old-style serif best communicate "establishment" for your startup? Is showcasing detailed product photography the best approach to attracting your audience? You'd be surprised how many clients prefer this approach to the fairly subjective "Pick your favorite of these three comps."

By removing the subjectivity, you can set the standard for rational intent early on. Not only is this helpful getting out of the gate, but it's arguably more so later in the project. If you acquiesce to a color shift out of personal preference in the beginning, it sets the precedent that such calls are acceptable later as well. Even the smallest tweak should have rationale that maps to user or organizational goals.

Asking Good Questions

In The Win Without Pitching Manifesto (*www.winwithoutpitching.com/ presentations-or-conversations*), Blair Enns writes, "We welcome the client's input on the strategy, and in exchange we ask him to grant us the freedom to explore various ways of executing it. This means we invite him to say, 'That blue isn't bold enough to deliver on our core value of strength.' But we explain that he is not invited to say, 'Make it darker.' Suggestions on this front are always welcome, but dictates are not."

The visual inventory approach brings our expertise with the Web into a veritable game of match-maker with the client's brand. We establish which directions are worth pursuing further without the guesswork of three flavors of mock-ups. What's more, we work with our clients collaboratively to figure this out in a way comps never could. Now comes the fun part: putting this feedback into pixels.

Conversations, Not Deliverables

The flaw with most design practices is inherent to the term *deliverable*. In a responsive workflow, the goal shouldn't be to continually deliver assets so a client can approve every phase, facsimile, and exercise. That's neither flexible nor practical. Everything we explore is valuable to the process, but no single item should be held as sacred.

Vetting direction isn't a deliverable. It's a conversation around the ideas you can put style to. A moodboard or a visual inventory may take the form of a document, but neither is meant to provide a direct representation of your site. Instead, they're meant to trigger important discussions that will influence the evolution of design throughout the entire project.

Why is this distinction important? Deliverables keep your stakeholders at a considerable distance from the inner workings of our processes. They also imply that you're providing specification, but in early ideation phases such as moodboards and visual inventories, you're not. Consequently, you're also not ideating in later stages of refinement, since you've explored potential paths early in the design process. Though the possibilities may be expansive early, the idea is to continually refine a solution the further you go.

Experimenting with Style

Moodboards or visual inventories should provide a loose set of parameters to start exploring style. In the next chapter, you'll see some exciting new methods for matching your brands to these directions and helping you establish a single direction to take to the browser.

6

ESTABLISHING STYLE

Think back to a time when your design process was fairly arbitrary. For you, it might be when you first started learning web design or perhaps when you went to work for yourself. In the first stages of a project, do you recall the anticipation of putting down the first pixels in Photoshop? Without the overhead of more structured processes, you'd be so excited just to start putting together the header and hero image for the homepage or start toying with how profile avatars and major call-to-action buttons would look.

Rarely does anyone get excited about designing footers, sidebar ad placement regions, or forms. But we must. In order to have accurate page designs, we need to show all the mundane details alongside the ones we're psyched about. The minutiae of a comp is the *lorem ipsum* to the eagerly conceived poetry we want to dive into.

What if I told you it's not only OK to plunge into designing only the stuff you're most excited about but doing so might be the catalyst for transforming your entire workflow?

In this chapter, you'll explore why.

Suitable Mock-up Replacements

While it's true that visual inventories are well worth exploring prior to producing full-page comps, you're much better off continuing with the idea of staying small and flexible. It's tempting to take what you've learned and spend a few weeks in Photoshop committing to your findings, but it's also risky. Not only might you be putting all your design-direction eggs in one basket, so to speak, but you'd still be susceptible to the pitfalls of the waterfall, full-page comp workflow described in previous chapters.

On Sketching

TIP If you haven't made sketching or sharing your sketches part of your process, I highly suggest you do so. I don't have the space in this chapter to cover an exhaustive exploration of sketching strategies, techniques, and materials, but you should pick up *Sketching User Experiences: The Workbook* by Saul Greenberg, Sheelagh Carpendale, Nicolai Marquardt, and Bill Buxton if you're interested in learning more.

You could take a rough approach to defining style, and you can't get much rougher in fidelity than paper-and-pencil/pen/marker sketches. As expressed earlier in a quote from Jason Dziak, sketching helps further the style conversation without committing to pixels (see **Figure 6.1**). The advantage here is keeping the art direction rough, which is a great strategy in the early stages of design.

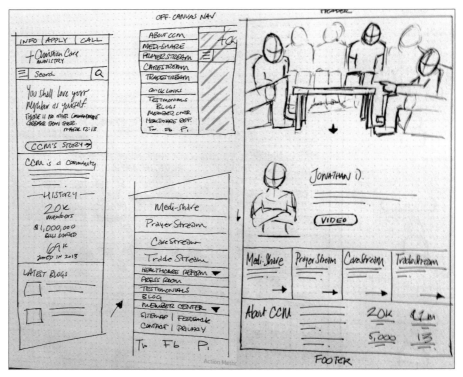

Figure 6.1 While sketching is great for exploring many ideas quickly, style-related exploration usually involves moving to higher-fidelity approaches.

Rough sketches often can't convey enough in terms of style. You can show shape, layout, and even some rudimentary type or color, but an exploration in higher fidelity is almost always necessary.

Fortunately, a number of talented folks have created approaches that reduce the scope of what we're designing while still supplying the detail we so desperately want to dive into.

Style Tiles

A popular alternative to full-page mock-ups is style tiles (*http://styletil.es/*), a term and exploration coined by Samantha Warren (see **Figure 6.2**).

> "Style tiles are similar to the paint chips and fabric swatches an interior designer gets approval on before designing a room. An interior designer doesn't design three different rooms for a client at the first kickoff meeting, so why do web designers design three different web page mock-ups?"
>
> —SAMANTHA WARREN (*http://styletil.es*)

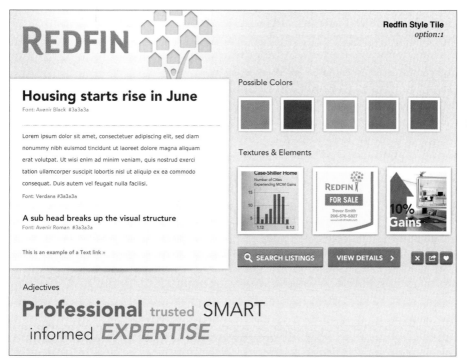

Figure 6.2 Style tiles have been widely adopted as a practical alternative to full-page comps.
SOURCE: WWW.THEARTISANVISUAL.COM

TIP You can download a blank style tile template from *http://styletil.es/ downloads/Style_Tile_ Template.psd.zip.*

A *style tile* is a Photoshop document that focuses on a few foundational elements to carry the visual theme of a website. Typically, these elements include the following:

▶ Basic typography (headings, paragraph text)

▶ A button or link style

▶ Primary color palette (three to five swatches)

▶ Possible patterns and backgrounds

▶ A list of adjectives (from which you derive design principles)

The best approach to setting up a style tile is open to interpretation. The sample provided on *http://styletil.es* is 1024x768, but don't let that discourage you from making it wider or taller. The only thing that should dissuade you from using a specific size is the device-independent focus of the practice. The goal is to define the basic visual language for a responsive site. Stacking the elements in a 320px width screen would inadvertently imply appearance in a narrow context like a smartphone.

Advantages of Style Tiles

Let's break down style tiles a bit further, starting with the advantages of using them. Primarily, style tiles achieve the goal of considerably stripping down the work we've traditionally done. A small sampling of the intended styles for a site essentially does the job of many large mock-ups.

As with the majority of full-page comp alternatives, style tiles cut down the number of hours spent in Photoshop at the beginning of a project while still accomplishing the goal of establishing the visual direction of a site. The benefit is that the saved budget and time can be better used addressing the complexities of variable-width layout in the browser.

One of the best benefits of style tiles is their versatility. It's quite easy to establish one theme, copy the file, and produce another. Little effort need be wasted as the foundational elements appear on each version, with the only changes being stylistic outside of changing adjectives. Whether you've started with a visual inventory or not, this is a great method of providing choice and comparison for our conversations. I'll cover the specific benefits of choice in Chapter 12.

Lastly, style tiles do the least to imply the most. For our purposes, it doesn't take very much for designers and developers alike to riff off the little we've established and create robust systems. Focusing on the building blocks of an interface gives us a great start for further implementation.

Exercise: Reverse-Engineer a Style Tile

If the idea of a style tile seems a bit wild to you, I've found the following exercise helpful in imagining their usefulness.

Begin by picking a website, preferably one you're familiar with—Apple, Target, Starbucks…whatever. Next, open the blank style tile template in Photoshop. Challenge yourself to fill in the blanks in what I like to call "reverse-engineering" a style tile. It's fascinating to see the building blocks of style in such a minimal form and how they can translate to a bigger design system. This practice should get you in the groove of what to include from the start (see Figure 6.3).

If you want to have some *real* fun, reverse-engineer a style tile, strip out the logo at the top, and quiz your designer friends to see whether they can guess what site you chose. It's so much fun you can hardly stand it, right?

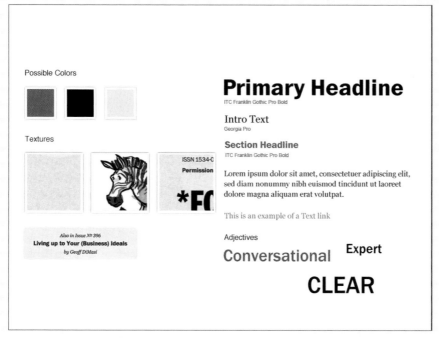

Figure 6.3 Any guess what site this comes from?

Style Prototypes

Do you like the style tile approach but wonder why it can't be done in the browser instead? My friends at Sparkbox (*www.seesparkbox.com*) have done just that with an approach called *style prototypes*.

There are a few differences between the two, but style prototypes (see **Figure 6.4**) are used for the same purpose as style tiles: to gain consensus on a design direction very early in the process without sacrificing the time and resources traditional mock-ups take.

Figure 6.4 Style prototypes bring the style tile conversation to the browser from the start. SOURCE: SPARKBOX

The clear advantage of using the browser as a design medium is the ability to work in responsive behavior. While the contents of a style prototype aren't meant to communicate a specific page layout, it might be helpful to begin to discuss how certain elements could adapt.

As relatively new as responsive web design is to us designers, it's even newer and often completely unfamiliar to our clients, which means we need to take every opportunity to weave in the concept. Even in a project's infancy, showing style in the browser may help familiarize your clients with this concept.

Flexibility by Design

In terms of content, the style prototype aligns well with the style tile, but it features some added flexibility by design.

"There's really no perfect set of design elements to include in a style prototype," says Sparkbox Creative Director Jeremy Loyd. "However, here are some basic elements to get you started:

▶ Branded header (with logo)

▶ Headline(s)

▶ Subhead(s)

▶ Paragraph style

▶ Button style (with hovers, transitions, etc.)

▶ Text link treatment

"I also like to include iconography, illustration, photo style, and any graphic patterns or textures," Loyd adds. "Navigation and UI elements for e-commerce or social networking may also be appropriate."

TIP No matter the deliverable, make sure you're showing it in the browser. If it's code-based, it'll naturally be there. If it's static, make a blank Hypertext Markup Language (HTML) page for it to live in. Why? The disconnect from an operating system's default JPEG viewer and the browser can be problematic in terms of zoom. Are you certain your design is being viewed at 100 percent? Why not have every possible discussion in the environment your design will end up living in, for consistency's sake?

Including elements like a header and navigation starts to bring us closer to what we've traditionally done in comps, clearing up some of the abstraction of how this translates to the actual site. How can we communicate style without "committing" to the detail and minutiae? I imagine the spectrum to be something like **Figure 6.5**.

Figure 6.5 While we've traditionally stayed too far on the right, more liberal approaches like style tiles can be a bit abstract. Style prototypes can bring us closer to the middle.

How far to the right style prototypes appear on this spectrum depends on you, your client's needs, and sometimes the budget for your project. At WSOL, we pushed this idea a bit further and included a few more components than normal, as shown in **Figure 6.6**.

Figure 6.6 On this project for Fuller Seminary, we used more defined elements to illustrate the style direction. As not to get too far into development, we opted to show a single breakpoint (width).

The flexibility is really up for interpretation. If building in more than one breakpoint seems arduous, it's totally acceptable to omit every intended breakpoint for the sake of discussion.

While it may appear that the style prototype approach is a browser-only exercise, I've found that doing some preliminary "sketches" in Photoshop helps aid in "what to show." Traditional low-fidelity sketching on paper works fine too, but the environment of Photoshop (and my efficiency in it) helps me think in terms of color, type, and layout better. Often, these Photoshop sketches are very loose and rarely shown to anyone, but they help address the "browser block" I experience, even at the style prototype level. I'll talk more about this in Chapter 8.

There are some things to watch out for when building style prototypes, with perhaps the most obvious being that it's easy to continually build components in an effort to better visualize the direction. You certainly don't want to make so many contributions to the style prototype that it could pass as the entire front end of your design.

On a similar note, using code that doesn't adhere to your team's production readiness isn't a deal-breaker, but it can cause some regret as you move toward site development needing to re-create elements in slightly more efficient or accurate code.

Style prototypes are a great step in the right direction. More flexible than style tiles, they can be interpreted and tweaked to best fit your team, clients, and projects. Even though Photoshop can be used to inspire them, style prototypes are HTML & CSS-centric, which may pose a stumbling block to the code-averse and the code-inefficient. In those cases, you'll want a developer taking the lead on implementing your design vision.

Component Inventory

Continuing along the spectrum toward "detailed" approaches, we end up with what I call component inventories. These are typically Photoshop documents that detail every element from which to build a site.

What style tiles and Prototypes might lack in literal translation to actual site elements, component inventories more than make up for through their sheer thoroughness and detail. If the goal is to outline every element on a site (or at least the majority of them), there's little chance you'll run into the abstraction problems of adjectives and pattern snippets.

Photoshop provides a rich environment to assess the range of styles on a given project. As one of the main objectives for the designer in this approach, systematic consistency comes into greater focus than it would in page mock-ups. Do I really need 15 button styles? Can I reduce six grays down to three?

Borrowing Character Styles from InDesign

A popular feature of InDesign has always been the ability to establish character styles. A *character style* outlines the size, color, and other attributes of type and allows you to quickly apply it where you'd like. Need to adjust every instance of Heading 1? It's easy-peasy in InDesign but not so much in Photoshop.

The good news is that character styles have made their way into Photoshop with the release of Creative Cloud. Here's how to access them:

1. Go to Window > Character Styles.

2. Choose the "Create new character style" icon located at the bottom of the panel. By default, a style called Character Style 1 appears.

3. Double-click Character Style 1 to begin assigning attributes. The dialog that appears also allows you to rename this style, which is pretty handy, as you can imagine.

TIP You can use multiple Photoshop CC libraries to quickly produce a few different iterations of the same elements.

Component inventories (see **Figure 6.7**) can take the same amount of time as full-page comps, making them dissimilar to previous, smaller-scope approaches. However, comps aren't exhaustive in the elements included over the span of a few page mock-ups, often leaving a significant number of components unconsidered. If the goal of each is to become a specification document, the more thorough component inventories have the advantage. All components will need to be figured out eventually. At the very least, component inventories take the same amount of time but allow you to use that time more wisely.

If you can work efficiently, component inventories are the best way of defining a style system prior to development.

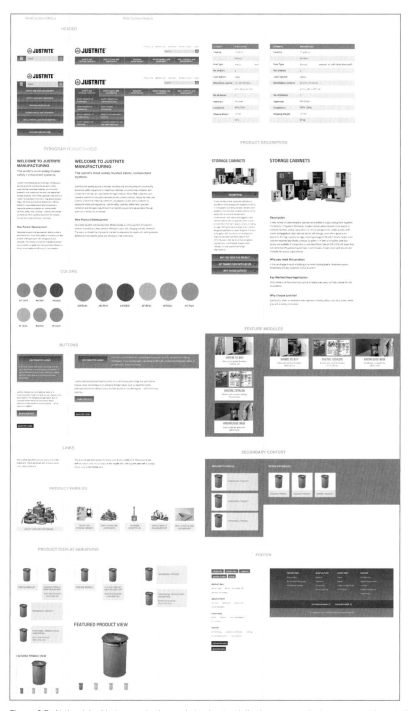

Figure 6.7 At the risk of being overly thorough (and potentially time-consuming), component inventories allow you to break down the elements of a site from within Photoshop.

Element Collages

Dan Mall created a mock-up alternative he calls *element collages* (see **Figure 6.8**). Done entirely in Photoshop, an element collage is a collection of visual ideas that represent potential site components. Like other methods, the goal is for these components to carry the essence of an entire theme.

Figure 6.8 An element collage might be the Photoshop-browser bridge you've been looking for.

Perhaps it's a collection of visual metaphors, like a social network showing a "post" with a paper-like container for the content or a sports site's live scores using the vernacular of a scoreboard's electronic numerals. These ideas have weight in our conversations, primarily because they *don't* deal with the minutiae of design. They center more around their applicability to a brand than their accuracy to a page.

If you set the expectation that these vignettes are your take at establishing some visual themes to continue on, the conversation becomes less about approval and more about fit. Sure, you can iterate on an element collage until you land on a handful of components you will produce to the pixel, more or less. But the fundamental idea here isn't that you need to work out every detail in Photoshop before moving to the browser. You can establish enough ideas to comprise a direction. The major advantage of element collages is that your ideas have detail, better informing the complete style direction and the choices you make in the browser.

Stripping Out the Abstraction

The main barrier the aforementioned deliverables present is abstraction. This is especially true of style tiles. Even style prototypes can require a considerable leap to "visualize" how they relate to a site. If you make verbose component inventories too early in an attempt to communicate design direction, it's often hard for clients to put together the pieces out of context.

Element collages, on the other hand, do a great job at balancing abstraction and detail (see **Figure 6.9**). Because you're designing at the component level, all of the examples shown are detailed, but they're also contextual because you're using "real" content. Simultaneously, element collages are still abstract in the sense that they aren't full-page designs or builds and often feature device frames and hands to further dissuade that notion. Less of a specification document than component inventories, element collages introduce ideas rather than refined solutions.

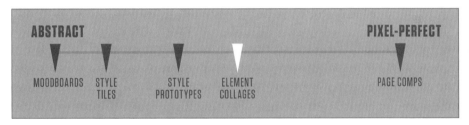

Figure 6.9 Our amended spectrum, where element collages are placed squarely between abstract and literal

All these ideas about element collages are fantastic, but I have a feeling you're itching to talk about the details of making them. So am I.

Crafting an Element Collage

Exercise time. Crack those knuckles and fire up Photoshop, if you please.

Canvas Size

First things first: What size do you make an element collage? Great question, and I can definitively say there's no single answer, by intention. The only difference between a 1800px wide document and a 1900px wide document is the number of ideas you can put into it. Let's run with that and start really big—annoyingly big. I think 3200px wide by 1800px tall should suffice.

Now what? Blank document syndrome, right? I tend to toss in some arbitrary guides to give myself at least one constraint to start. I do this using GuideGuide, which you'll explore in Chapter 10. What's most important is to not predefine any of the popular device sizes, such as putting guides at 0 and 1024. You want to break out of the habit of designing for specific screens (unless your project is a native app). Users will view your designs on any number of devices, so it's irresponsible to focus only on the ones you might have or think of.

Turning Powerful Phrases Into Visual Hooks

For me, it helps to start thinking about phrases I've heard in discovery and kickoff meetings. To escape the "sameness" of contemporary web style, descriptive terms unique to your clients and their industries can provide a way.

One WSOL client, Christian Care Ministry (CCM), is a community deeply rooted on the concept of sharing resources, both spiritual and physical. Their mission is to further the gospel message by harboring a "tight-knit" community. We heard this phrase throughout our initial meetings with them, and though the copy and photos of the site aim to communicate it, we thought, why not incorporate these ideas into the interface as well? Including this background pattern on the element collage was a way to kick-start a conversation about using even the most subtle of hints to portray their mission (see **Figure 6.10**). For the 5 to 10 percent of viewers who pick up that this woven pattern relates to the community, it's worth it.

Dan Mall refers to this technique as "turning powerful phrases into visual hooks." **Figure 6.11** shows an example he provides from a project done for Reading is Fundamental, transforming a phrase like "Turn to page 2" into an interface element.

Not only is this a great strategy for establishing some semblance of uniqueness, but it can also help kick-start the art direction. An approach to style should go beyond flat or skeuomorphic, shallow or deep. You can use key phrases from your clients to influence the interface in a meaningful way, creating opportunities to evaluate how their brand can be represented beyond a logo or some text.

When done tastefully and cleverly, visual metaphors are a great foundation for an element collage and web design in general.

TIP It's possible this scale is more than just uncomfortable for you; it's inconvenient. No sweat. You can adjust it to whatever fits your screen or current setup. The idea is that you don't want to start at 960px or 1024x768 (or any "standard" device size). You can always add more canvas or take it away later. Ideally, a feature like Adobe Illustrator's artboards would be great here, but a large canvas should suffice.

Figure 6.10 Homing in on key phrases and creating their graphic equivalent can produce some unique results.

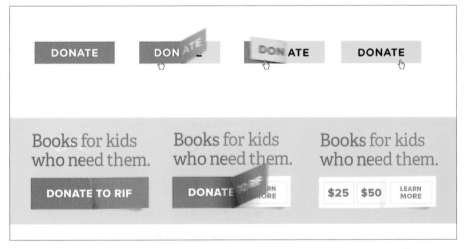

Figure 6.11 A superb example of taking the vernacular of a company or industry and translating it to UI
SOURCE: SUPERFRIENDLY

Covering a Lot of Ground Quickly

Adjusting the scope of Photoshop comping is critical to a responsive project, where the time and budget savings can be used elsewhere. Beyond showing metaphors, it's worth your while to explore the components whose style can best represent the direction you're exploring. Including interface elements like buttons can inspire how other links and utilities will eventually be styled. Similarly, while you may be placing your artwork on a white canvas, crafting backgrounds for related content blocks set the expectation that your sections will have variety (see **Figure 6.12**).

Figure 6.12 It would behoove you to mix in elements that can do the heavy lifting of conveying a theme.

Each project is different, so it's up to you to determine which components can do the heavy lifting. It could be headlines, accordions, tabs, photo galleries, or forms. Who knows? You're only a border, notch, or drop cap away from creating a signature pattern worth reusing throughout the design.

An important part of the shift from showing one direction to showing a few is proper setup. In the past, designers may have introduced multiple mock-ups as "options," implying that one is better than the others and the others will be discarded. Instead, multiple directions within element collages don't necessarily imply that all but one gets trashed. Redeeming qualities from less successful directions can still influence the end result.

With iterative design, your aim is to work toward a convergence of refining a solution. For CCM's element collage, I described two directions for how we could execute their primary navigation: one bright but heavy and the other light but lesser in character. Although at the beginning of the conversation we collectively opted for the heavier option, CCM noted the value of the light option as something not to throw out entirely. It wasn't until we were in the latter stages of designing a high-fidelity prototype in the browser that we recognized that the visual heaviness of the navigation outweighed its charm. Instead of defaulting to using our second exploration, we determined a way to adjust the first with the essence of the second (see **Figure 6.13**).

Figure 6.13 The progression of CCM's header style, which ultimately used traits from both element collages

I mentioned that we presented two ideas for navigation style. For the components you want to show variations of, I recommend showing them in the same element collage. With the old methodology, in which each style direction had its own file, you could show two versions of an element in two files. But keep in mind that you aren't presenting a complete direction for approval anymore. Hence, you need not isolate one version in an environment uncontaminated from another.

In fact, showing a client two versions of an element juxtaposed against each other is the most natural way to assess their value. The talented design studio Clearleft takes this approach in its impressively exhaustive element collages (see **Figure 6.14**). As designer Jon Aizlewood notes, including variation isn't just about providing choice:

> ❝As far as its size, secretly I enjoy doing element collages more than detailed UI page design because they let you iterate through lots of different ideas quickly. You can avoid the standard constraints like screen sizes and page layouts and simply chuck things onto a canvas and see what works best.❞
>
> —JON AIZLEWOOD

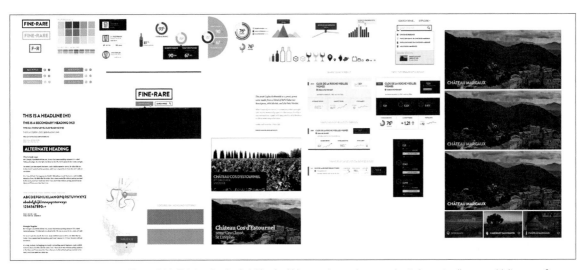

Figure 6.14 This is a lovely sketchbook of ideas and a much more robust element collage, wouldn't you say?
SOURCE: CLEARLEFT

Do Not Make It Look Like a Website

The risk we run in making comps like style tiles and element collages is that they can easily look like a website. *But isn't it supposed to look like a website, you ask? Aren't we, um, making websites?*

Sorta. First, allow me to explain why they might look like a website so easily. Full-page comping has trained us to work on canvases taller than they are wide. Heck, the Web is generally taller than it is wide. Naturally, when we begin stacking elements vertically, the composition begins to look like a website even if it's not our intention. Clearleft ran into this problem when they presented the element collage shown in **Figure 6.15**.

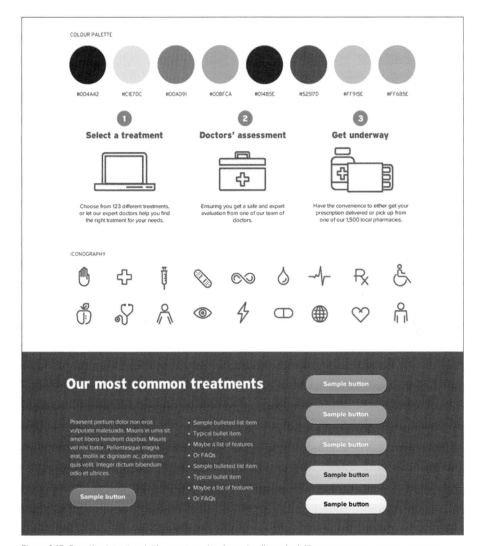

Figure 6.15 Even if unintentional, it's easy to make element collages look like page comps. SOURCE: CLEARLEFT

At a very quick glance it's easy to mistake this collage for an actual page.

To circumvent this problem, Clearleft started laying out element collages extremely wide. Rarely would you meet someone who expects to scroll horizontally on a site, so it helped distinguish that this is a collection of ideas versus a specific page. Would you believe that sometimes that's still not enough?

There are a few more things that can be done. We've started to show layouts in generic device frames right on the collage (see **Figure 6.16**).

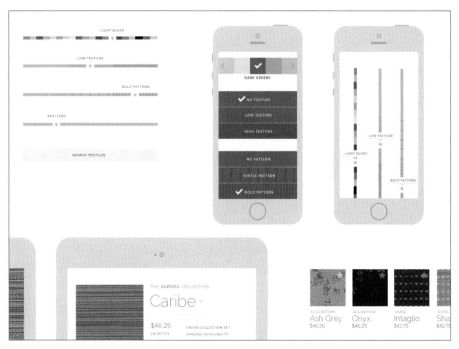

Figure 6.16 Nobody would realistically expect these devices to appear within page content, so they make great frames for our collaging.

The thought is that a client wouldn't expect to see these kind of devices framing their content within the context of a page, unless you were pitching an app *per se*. Dan Mall takes this a step further and often shows actual hands holding real devices (see **Figure 6.17**).

It's wise to consider any and every avenue that properly distances your collage from a page comp. Although you may still need to disclaimer your approach, avoiding confusion at this stage is critical.

Figure 6.17 A helping hand, if I ever saw one

Color Comparisons

A common exploration request during style ideation is to see how different color schemes would look applied to content. I've long contended that color is just as easy to explore in Photoshop than the browser, if not easier, given that the scope is small. Obviously, if you wanted to see how a shift in blue would affect multiple pages or elements, CSS is the way to go. If you want to shift the blue on a button or single instance, Photoshop is arguably your best bet.

Pittsburgh design shop Bearded has used element collages to assess color scheme (see **Figure 6.18**).

Figure 6.18 Publishing a few different color options with the same components can make for easy assessment.
SOURCE: BEARDED

I hope you're seeing how versatile element collages can be, given their smaller scope than traditional comps. You do plan on limiting the scope, right?

Scope Creep

I probably don't have to explain how easy it is to go overboard designing element collages. They can quickly become detailed component libraries if you're not careful. What starts out as an exploration of a few visual metaphors, navigation items, and buttons can grow into an exhaustive exercise in accounting for *every* interface element.

The chief reason why you want to avoid designing exhaustive systems in Photoshop is predicated on the "double effort" theory described in Chapter 2. Whatever you do in Photoshop will ultimately need to be redone in code.

Where do you draw the line? I'm not sure there's a great answer that's widely applicable, but I've always tried to imply the most by designing the least (see **Figure 6.19**). If you can communicate a complete design direction by presenting a few components, you've done your job. If you have to execute 90 percent of the components to illustrate a direction, you're probably in the "too much effort" zone.

Figure 6.19 Some projects need very little to convey design direction.

The inclusion of too many components can occur because of your own inclination or the request of your client. Either way, it's a type of "scope creep" that you need to protect against. Element collages, like any other post-full-page comp strategy, need to be efficient. If it turns into another "Photoshop phase," you've lost one of its main advantages.

Additionally, if there's no cap on exploration, how can you accurately price what it will cost? You may not have to put a hard number such as 30 hours or $5,000 on element collages, but it's irresponsible to imply that they'll be an efficient part of the process and then turn around and spend the majority of the project budget on them. Everyone is different, so I won't suggest a number of hours or rate you should charge for element collaging. However, it may take you a time or two to begin pricing them with accuracy.

Asking the Right Questions

As you saw with visual inventories, a major part of being successful in a responsive process is knowing how to ask the right questions. Structuring your conversations around useful feedback is the secret sauce to a successful project. If you fail to receive input from your clients, you can't build out a design system with any more confidence than what you had prior to the exercise.

Let's start with what not to ask: "Which one do you like better?"

> " The client didn't hire you to make something they liked, and something they like may not be the thing that leads to their success. So do not conflate the two. This point needs to be driven home from the very beginning of the project. And nowhere is this message more undermined than using language that leads them down a subjective path. "
>
> —MIKE MONTEIRO (*https://medium.com/@monteiro/13-ways-designers-screw-up-client-presentations-51aaee11e28c*)

The previous question (and variations of it) does little to give you any useful input moving forward. Unless mapped to specific user objectives, clients will typically have a difficult time responding completely objectively. What's worse, you'll probably start down a road of refining a solution until they are fully subjectively satisfied with what they see.

That's not what element collages, style tiles, or style prototypes are about. They're about aligning visual ideas with a brand and its message in an effort to kick-start a direction. Said direction is further explored and implemented in the browser because that's where you need to spend the bulk of your time in a responsive process. Refining an idea in Photoshop until it's approved is the antithesis of what you want to accomplish.

Instead, you want to ask better questions:

▶ How do you anticipate your end users would respond to this color/metaphor/direction?

▶ What kind of adjectives would you use to describe what you're seeing?

▶ You stated you wanted your brand to align to [insert trait]. Which collage (or variation) is more successful in that regard?

The answers to these types of questions can help in the long run, well after you're in the browser, filling out the design. The most important move you can make isn't crafting clever questions that no one has asked your clients before but identifying the objective user and organizational goals, scenarios, and design principles before you ask anything at all. These items are critical to establish and necessary for challenging an element collage against.

Do Make It Look Like a Website

You also want to temper the expectation that any feedback received will be immediately applied to the element collage. Just as in the visual inventory, lead your client to anticipate how a direction will manifest in the final design: *We'll still be exploring, but it will be helpful to know if we're on track with this approach.* Remember, you're looking for encouragement for the course of your design, not hard approval.

Arguably the best response will sound like this: "We understand there's more to work out, but we'd be thrilled if our site was in this flavor."

This response isn't exclusive to your clients, either. It's just as applicable to you and your team. If you can't see how an element collage translates to a finished website, perhaps you need to include different or additional components.

Point of Reference

Responsive design can get messy. I don't mean just in terms of components breaking from time to time; there are often situations where a lot of detail and focus gets put on one facet and not another.

For example, you may spend a good deal of time fine-tuning an off-canvas navigation function while overlooking the style of it. Perhaps it's a component like tabs, something you bake into most projects and don't give two thoughts about how to approach it any differently than the last time. Not only can this lead you into the trap of leaving some elements more considered than others, but it can quickly breed inconsistency in your UI.

For the record, I'm a staunch advocate of "working things" being superior to "pretty things." Yet I've also found that later on in the workflow, when some facets could use a little TLC, it helps to look back to what was established in the element collage as inspiration. If you establish it as a document to truly carry the design direction, it *probably* makes sense to go back and look at it every now and then. I'm guiltier than most at establishing these kind of documents early and disregarding them later only to bang my head against my keyboard trying to ideate solely using CSS.

Just because you don't have pixel-perfect mock-ups to provide a front-end development road map doesn't mean element collages can't be a valuable point of reference. They can and will if you continue to allow them to influence the entire design system moving forward. In fact, they also double as a great point of reference for your clients.

When questions do arise later, or differing opinions come into play, use the conversation that occurred around the element collage as a point of reference. For example, a stakeholder wants to change the hero image on the homepage to be a carousel of marketing news. This happens on every project, if you haven't already established a carousel of marketing news as the prime element on the homepage. You could use user research, information architecture documents, and usability studies to support keeping it a static image instead of a rotating one, and you should.

You also have the element collage to point to: *In the context of everything else we've explored here, we need the hero image to make a strong impact visually. Our concern is that we'll only weaken its presentation by splitting its content up five times.*

Where you may have created a component like this as a visual cornerstone of a direction, allow the element collage to support adhering to the spirit in which it was established. This helps communicate why breaking it up into five slides would be a departure not worth exploring.

I Still Can't See It

You can follow everything in this chapter to the letter and produce a gorgeous element collage and still find yourself being asked to put together a page mock-up. You can communicate the disadvantages of full-page comps and still be requested to provide them. Don't feel discouraged; this is normal! Why? Because responsive design is still new to all of us, and sometimes it's hard to transition to a different workflow that everyone feels confident in.

So comp. Mock up any page or width that your team or clients are having trouble visualizing, as long as you have the time. I'll even go further to say you *should* comp any page or part of a page you're having trouble with yourself (see **Figure 6.20**). Do it for yourself.

The difference here is found in the purpose. If you're being exhaustive with full-page comping and using them to gain approval, it sets up some faulty expectations down the road. But if, instead, you use them as high-fidelity sketches to better visualize how a page, or part of a page, can come together, there's little harm in this type of exploration.

There was a time where I had settled on firmly banishing page comps altogether. I've since noticed that might have been a bit rash and shortsighted. Yes, you can comp, but try to do so as efficiently and behind the scenes as you can.

Another strategy I've found helpful is to pair the presentation of an element collage with a gray-box, low-fidelity HTML prototype. The element collage acts as the inspiration for the style to eventually be applied to the prototype's layout. Often what's not being vocalized in these situations is that someone is having trouble visualizing the *layout* of the site if it's not established yet. A simple prototype can supply enough layout intention without the fine-tuning of polished functionality.

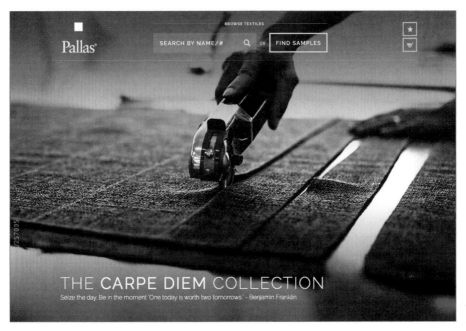

Figure 6.20 | needed to be confident the top of this homepage would come together, so I made a comp. No big deal!

What's Missing

Now you've thoroughly vetted inspiration with visual inventories and ideation with element collages. Unfortunately, a responsive website you do not have. To quote the inimitable Bon Jovi, "We're halfway there."

Now it's time to hop back out of Photoshop and into the browser for the nitty-gritty part of responsive web design: building the system.

7

ESTABLISHING THE SYSTEM

Between moving from an apartment to a house and having a second child, my wife and I have been in constant upgrade mode in terms of home furnishings. It's a funny stage—you want better furniture than you came out of college with, but with children you can't afford to be too particular. Take it from me, yet-to-be-parents: Crayon and food stains will abound.

The best option for us continues to be IKEA. If you've been there, you're familiar with the craziness that ensues while trekking the showroom. There are tons of home goods to choose from, and the enormity of the place makes it all but impossible to walk away with any fewer than five purchases. Living in Syracuse, New York, only compounds the matter: The closest IKEA is five hours in any direction.

Because of the distance, we always feel compelled to make the most of the pilgrimage. Our last trip was quite a haul. I'm fairly certain we've mastered the art of stuffing their iconic flat boxes into SUVs. Each item is packed in a nondescript and minimally shaped cardboard box, or series of boxes, and convenience comes at a price: Assembling IKEA furniture is a bit like building your house out of Legos. It's achievable, but it's going to cost you a few weekends.

Having built cribs, tables, dressers, and chairs over the years, I'd like to consider myself an aficionado of sorts when it comes to IKEA products and assembly. Probably the smartest thing about their products are the shared parts across various lines. Open any product, and you will inevitably find the same dowels, cams, and pins. Rarely do you find a part that's a one-off and never used on a different piece of furniture.

That's the idea we're aiming for in component-based design: reusability and consistency. With it, your design will be cohesive across widths and pages. Without it, you'll have a collection of limited and inflexible one-off pieces that are difficult to scale across widths and pages. It's always a good idea to take inventory of all your pieces before you start building.

Now It's the Browser's Turn

As promised, we're weaving between Photoshop and code again. Unlike waterfall processes that separate design and development, we can start development even while element collage explorations are happening. When you start overlapping design with development, you'll find it's a fairly wild concept that will take extra communication if you're not the one doing both tasks.

There are three pieces of in-browser design I want to tackle. The first is creating a *style guide*, where you outline the foundational elements of your site. The next step is crafting a *component library* to house all the reusable patterns and modules you'll be deploying. Lastly, you'll put it all together in a *high-fidelity prototype* that should resemble the polished site or templates you've been working toward.

Defining the Style Guide

You may be familiar with the term *style guide* from a traditional application. In print, a style guide is a document (typically printed or PDF) containing any and all of a company's identity guidelines. *The logo should have X amount of space around it. The Pantone value for our yellow is 109. Our corporate typeface is Gotham.*

Traditional style guides are often distributed by the brand police in hopes of maintaining consistency in various applications (see **Figure 7.1**). Naturally, it's been common practice to include some guidelines for web contexts, though it's here you'll often find some misguided input. For example, a style guide established for a company in 2005 will most likely point out that the corporate typeface for web use is Arial. It might even define a "web-safe" color palette. Other times you'll simply find rules and regulations for the Web made by someone who doesn't have working knowledge of its freedoms and constraints. That's when things get really fun.

You needn't spend a moment attempting to correct inaccuracies in the little space devoted to the Web in a print manual. Instead, you can, and should, build a style guide in HTML & CSS that can be a resource not just after site launch but during the fulfillment of the design process.

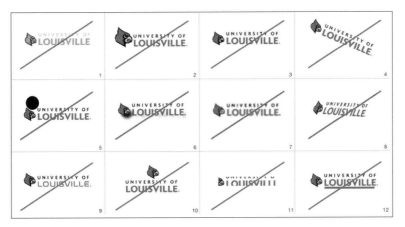

Figure 7.1 Traditional style guides focus on brand do's and don'ts, like Louisville's logo guidelines.
SOURCE: UNIVERSITY OF LOUISVILLE

Web-Specific

A web-specific style guide is a reference document that outlines any rules for elements to be used by content authors. To better illustrate what's included, here's a list to get you started:

▶ Colors

▶ Typography

▶ Link styles

▶ Buttons

▶ Tables

▶ Image formats

▶ Icons

The following sections give a more detailed breakdown of those elements.

Colors

An intentional, systematic color palette should sit at the foundation of your design. In the most practical sense, knowing what's the "official" blue and the variations of it can only be a good thing for everyone to adhere to.

My general rule of thumb is to define at least three colors and their variations (see **Figure 7.2**). For example, our primary color here is purple, with lighter and darker shades for use in behaviors such as hover interactions. A secondary color is established, usually in the same warmness or coolness of the primary. In this case, it's blue. A tertiary or accent color, while used sparingly, will help define areas of contrast or action. We've chosen orange.

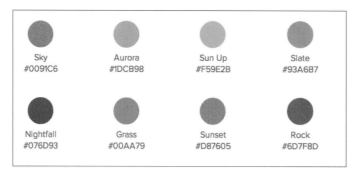

Figure 7.2 It's always helpful to show swatches alongside color information.

I've found it helpful to display a swatch (a square div with a background-color) as well as the color name, hierarchy, and hex value. Assigning each color a name helps when referencing it in casual conversation. It's the Crayola thing to do, right? A color's hierarchy is helpful in CSS: Classes of "primary/secondary/tertiary" give good indication of use without the pitfall of naming something ".purple," only for it to change to red later.

The more carefully you set up color in CSS, the easier it is to change it globally. To change all the instances of purple to blue across Photoshop comps is a terribly inefficient task. This is an area where designing in the browser and setting up a system in the browser has a major advantage over traditional Photoshop page comp methods.

Lastly, the hex value is great for copy and pasting. If you want to be really thorough, RGB may prove to be an even better option for incorporating alpha transparency (RGBA). All in all, defining colors through CSS provides a reference point in the HTML style guide and should crack down on the inadvertent "close-to-but-not-quite" variations of base colors typically found in Photoshop comps.

Typography

When it comes to including type, think in terms of what styles a content author would be choosing between (see **Figure 7.3**). Naturally, headings, paragraph/body text, block quotes, introductory text, labels, and lists are great to include here. It's helpful to wrangle up and audit all the typographic variations throughout a website. The beauty of this type inventory is that it reveals redundant or slightly similar styles you can combine.

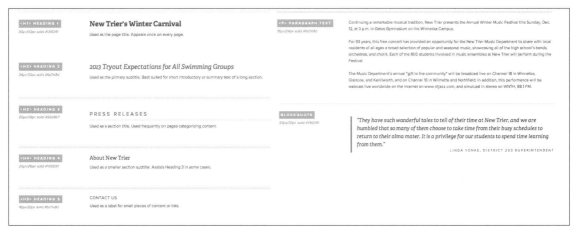

Figure 7.3 As the foundation of any website, be sure to include basic typography styles in your style guide.

Link Styles

What might take three instances in Photoshop can be achieved in a single interactive instance in code (see **Figure 7.4**). Provide an example of an inline link and assign it default, active, visited, and hover state values. It's not important to provide other link formats that rely on components such as navigation or menus, as you'll add those elsewhere. Don't forget to specify how headings look when linked.

> For more information about this event, **get in touch** with Peter Tragos.

Figure 7.4 Don't go too far down a design without considering the humble inline link.

Buttons

When you designed page comps, how easy was it to make 1,000 button iterations? It was incredibly easy, because each button was generally styled to the content surrounding it. By declaring a few button styles here, you'll try to mitigate the need for hundreds of slightly different button styles, which can be confusing to your users (see **Figure 7.5**). Your goal in specifying button styles should be consistency: Does every button's hover get darker or lighter?

Figure 7.5 It's wise to have only a few sizes and styles of buttons.

Tables

Tables are another element native to most CMS text editors but easily overlooked by designers. Browser-default table styles are usually horrid, so make sure you show them some love in the style guide (see **Figure 7.6**). More importantly, tables are usually one of the most difficult elements to display legibly on narrow screens, so the effort to address them at this stage in the game is worth your while.

REGULAR TABLE				
ATHLETE	YEAR	SCORE	PLACE	OPPONENT
George White	Sophomore	93.3	1st	Grayson Samuels
Tammy Banks	Junior	87.5	2nd	Jackie Franklin
Michael Thompson	Junior	87.2	3rd	Clint Barton
Jessica Wilthorpe	Senior	85.5	4th	Melinda Zurowski
Wilson Gutierrez	Freshman	82.9	5th	Lyle Hansel

Figure 7.6 Formatting table headings, cell padding, and text alignment can go a long way to making default tables look considered.

Image Dimensions

Another common task for content authors is placing images inside page content. I've had countless clients send panicked emails asking what they need to do to get a photo to fit correctly. You can help make their life easier by documenting the ratios and preferred dimensions in your style guide.

Icons

With the onset of icon fonts, it's never been easier to place icons on the Web. This last one isn't a necessity, but if you have icons that can be easily placed in content through a CMS, providing some syntax on your style guide is a good idea (see **Figure 7.7**).

TIP Alongside all of the aforementioned elements, I've also found it helpful to document a respective use case. For example, "Primary buttons are used only for major actions, such as downloading our app."

ICON	CLASS	ICON	CLASS
Home	.icon-home	Talk	.icon-bubble
News	.icon-newspaper	User	.icon-user
Edit	.icon-pencil	Users	.icon-users
Photo	.icon-camera	Menu	.icon-menu
YouTube	.icon-play	Link	.icon-link
Video	.icon-film	Star	.icon-star
File	.icon-file	No/Cancel/Close	.icon-close
File2	.icon-file2	Yes/Complete	.icon-checkmark
File3	.icon-file3	Less/Close	.icon-minus
Ticket	.icon-ticket	More/Open	.icon-plus
Contact	.icon-address-book	Notification	.icon-notification
Email	.icon-envelop	Go	.icon-play2
Location	.icon-location	Facebook	.icon-facebook
Time	.icon-clock	Google+	.icon-google-plus
Print	.icon-print	Twitter	.icon-twitter
Calendar	.icon-calendar	RSS	.icon-feed
Phone	.icon-mobile	Vimeo	.icon-vimeo
Download	.icon-download	Flickr	.icon-flickr
Upload	.icon-upload	LinkedIn	.icon-linkedin
Redo	.icon-redo	PDF	.icon-file-pdf

Figure 7.7 It's easy to include tons of icons, so just make sure each has a deliberate function.

Why the Style Guide Should Live in the Browser

You can create your style guide in Photoshop, and for some teams it may be easiest to do so. However, if the goal is to create a reference for content authors, a PSD or static image won't provide an ideal level of accessibility. If your author does not have Photoshop, they won't be able to extract text to copy to their clipboard. Code-based style guides shine in these areas.

HTML style guides also allow you to tweak values responsively. If you define text as 22px for wide views, you'll most likely want to adjust it to 16px or so for narrower ones. Depending on screen width, buttons might need less padding, lists might need more, and tables might take a completely different format.

The style guide is a perfect example of a "deliverable" that requires a "keep going" response rather than "final approval." As you continue to define the site design, chances are you'll be tweaking some values here or adding a few more buttons and image formats. The occasional gut-check is more than welcome through the creation of the guide, but it's hard to say you're ever complete until the site launches. Even then, an argument can be made that it should be updated when needed.

To recap, here's what you have in your design arsenal so far:

▶ Inspiration (visual inventory)

▶ Ideas (element collage)

▶ Base styles (style guide)

Only two tasks separate you from completing the design. Let's knock them out.

Building the Component Library

Comedian Jim Gaffigan has this really great bit about the questions he would have to answer as a waiter at a non-authentic Mexican restaurant:

"Hey, what's nachos?"

"Nachos? They're tortillas with cheese, meat, or vegetables."

"Ah. And what's a burrito?"

"That's a tortilla with cheese, meat, or vegetables."

"What's a tostada?"

"Tortilla with cheese, meat, or vegetables."

"What's a taco?"

…and so on.

That may or may not be your experience with Mexican food, but regardless, it's a shining example of using similar elements to compose (arguably) different components. This strategy has a clear parallel to interface design, in that it's advantageous to build out the pieces of a site within the constraints of a system rather than one-off ideas. Even if a burrito is the only dish with guacamole (it's not), the rest of the ingredients are familiar and consistent.

For responsive web design, the collection of menu items (Mexican dishes, in this example) we're looking to prepare is commonly called a *component* (or *pattern*) *library*. This document picks up from what you established in the style guide and fills out the remainder of what you'll need to start building pages.

Fair warning: This is where the bulk of your "designing" will occur.

Let's take a look at some common components to include:

▶ Forms and inputs

▶ Image grids

▶ Media blocks

▶ Hero blocks

▶ Figure with caption

▶ Primary calls-to-action

▶ Sign-up modules

▶ Navigation

▶ Sidebar callouts

▶ Breadcrumbs

▶ Pagination

▶ Tabbed panels

▶ Expandable panels

▶ Comments

▶ Alerts

▶ Latest/recent feeds

There are certainly more, depending on your project's needs, but I've found these to be a reliable representation of what it typically takes to build a page. For instance, you may be building a retail/e-commerce site and choose to include some product detail components such as the thumbnail, title, and price grouping. You may have a robust event listing module, a scoreboard, or a video block for each tutorial. Add those patterns to your document as well, and keep an eye out for any other reusable components.

Contents of a Comprehensive Component Library

Let's look at the essential components of the component library in a bit more depth.

Forms and Inputs

Just about every site has a need for user inputs such as text fields, check boxes, and radio buttons. It's handy to spec out the styling for just about any form element ahead of time so you'll have them ready when needed (see **Figure 7.8**). I typically forget to include `<select>` drop-downs and various input types (email, date, and so on), only to have to go back and include them later. It's also wise to be proactive about focus states, error states, and validation.

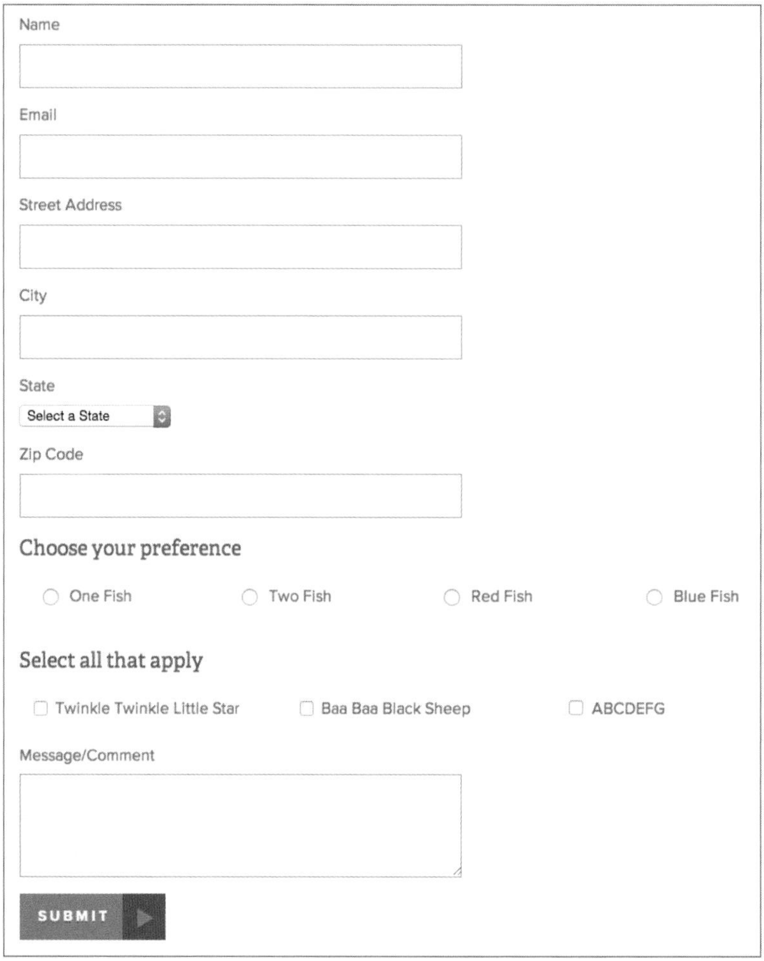

Name

Email

Street Address

City

State
Select a State

Zip Code

Choose your preference

○ One Fish   ○ Two Fish   ○ Red Fish   ○ Blue Fish

Select all that apply

☐ Twinkle Twinkle Little Star   ☐ Baa Baa Black Sheep   ☐ ABCDEFG

Message/Comment

SUBMIT ▶

Figure 7.8 A well-designed form doesn't just look nice but also has usability benefits.

Image Grids

Does your site use images? Great, so does mine! Even if you think you won't need a fluid grid of 20+ photos, I recommend setting up rules for one anyway. The idea here is to specify image blocks in terms of the space they require, such as two-up, three-up, four-up, and so on. This will allow easier layout options as you build pages.

Media Blocks

In this case, the term *media* refers to a generic left-right grouping of image and text. Common examples of this component include news items, product information, or profile details each offset by a thumbnail or avatar (see **Figure 7.9**). While they may be part of a bigger list, be sure to outline the details at the component level.

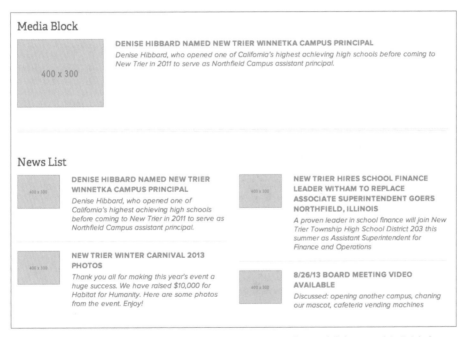

Figure 7.9 Image and text blocks like these are fairly common on most sites, so defining a consistent style for them is important.

Hero Blocks

It's hard to think of a site that doesn't have a large banner image or rotator sitting in the front seat of its homepage nowadays (see **Figure 7.10**). Even though it may appear to be a single-use component, you may end up choosing to use it on interior pages in a smaller format, making it worthy of inclusion in the component library.

Figure 7.10 Large banner images are a staple of many sites.

Figure with Caption

Unconsidered, an in-body-text photo with a small caption underneath is easily achieved by a content author in a what-you-see-is-what-you-get (WYSIWYG) editor (see **Figure 7.11**). Might you want to fancy it up a bit with a background or border containing both elements? How about overlaying the caption on top of the image with a slightly opaque background color? Considerations such as these are fruitful ones and should be documented here.

Figure 7.11 Well-defined image and caption combinations are easy to spot.

Primary Calls-to-Action

Perhaps your site has articles that end with instructions or a call-to-action button (see **Figure 7.12**). These typically have a different look from the default text and (occasionally) button style or size, and the component may be offset by a border or background.

Figure 7.12   Clear calls-to-action help direct users through your site.

Sign-up Modules

I discussed forms and inputs earlier, but there are some cases where you may want a special arrangement such as a search field and button or, for example, a newsletter sign-up that has instruction and icons (see **Figure 7.13**). Either pattern is great to include here because they're typically used across all pages of a site.

Figure 7.13   The components look nice, but there's nothing to group or frame them.

Navigation

There are many types of navigation: primary, secondary, main, utility, off-canvas, overlay, drop-down, footer, section, sidebar, interior, and audience (see **Figure 7.14**). You may deploy one or all of the above on your site, so collect them here. Though the primary objective is to provide a good bird's-eye view of style, it may also reveal any instances of link duplication.

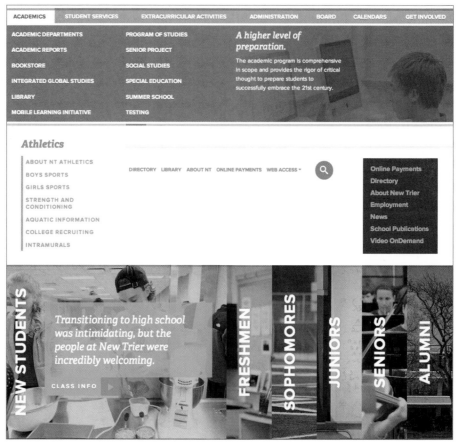

Figure 7.14 Navigation can take many shapes and forms, so it's best to collect each one in your component library.

Sidebar Callouts

Sidebars are prime areas for calling out related actions to a page's main content (see **Figure 7.15**). Examples of these callouts include a text, image, and button grouping or a list of links (associative navigation). By defining a system of these modules, you'll likely mitigate the need for one-off designs for each different callout, which can start to make your site look like a circus.

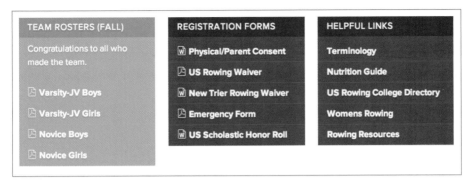

Figure 7.15 The components look nice, but there's nothing to group or frame them.

Breadcrumbs

Technically another piece of navigation, breadcrumbs (crumb trail) are a horizontal list usually found near the top of a page (see **Figure 7.16**). Be sure to account for them here.

HOME / EXTRACURRICULAR ACTIVITIES / ATHLETICS

Figure 7.16 Breadcrumb navigation is a great wayfinding component.

Pagination

Often lost in the sea of to-dos for me is styling pagination (see **Figure 7.17**). It's never the sexiest component, nor one that even comes to mind until I see it unstyled in development. Don't be like me. Give consideration ahead of time to any instances of pagination you plan on using in your project.

Figure 7.17 Often an oversight, pagination links can bear a lot of the same styles you've established with inline links or buttons.

Tabbed Panels

Tabbed panels (*tabs* for short) are the fast food of components (see **Figure 7.18**). They offer convenience for authors since they tuck away a good deal of content while still making it accessible through tab navigation. However, that tab navigation isn't always the prettiest thing to look at, especially in responsive contexts where the labels get smushed and crunched. It's kind of like that smushed Big Mac you get when you were expecting the statuesque version from the commercials. On narrow screens, you may opt to display all the tab content instead of hiding it.

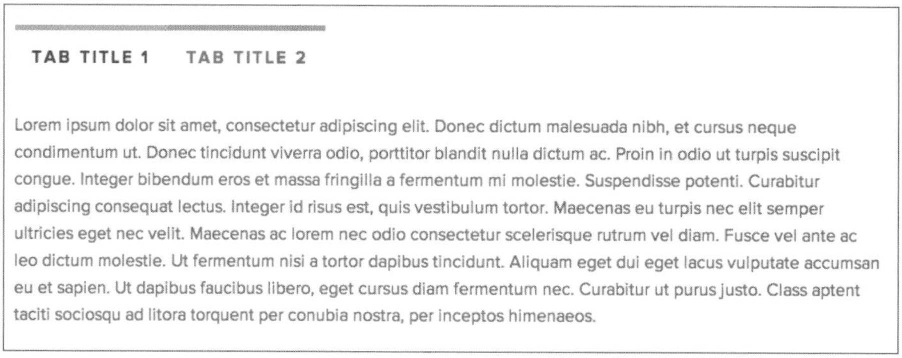

TAB TITLE 1
TAB TITLE 2
Lorem ipsum dolor sit amet, consectetur adipiscing elit. Donec dictum malesuada nibh, et cursus neque condimentum ut. Donec tincidunt viverra odio, porttitor blandit nulla dictum ac. Proin in odio ut turpis suscipit congue. Integer bibendum eros et massa fringilla a fermentum mi molestie. Suspendisse potenti. Curabitur adipiscing consequat lectus. Integer id risus est, quis vestibulum tortor. Maecenas eu turpis nec elit semper ultricies eget nec velit. Maecenas ac lorem nec odio consectetur scelerisque rutrum vel diam. Fusce vel ante ac leo dictum molestie. Ut fermentum nisi a tortor dapibus tincidunt. Aliquam eget dui eget lacus vulputate accumsan eu et sapien. Ut dapibus faucibus libero, eget cursus diam fermentum nec. Curabitur ut purus justo. Class aptent taciti sociosqu ad litora torquent per conubia nostra, per inceptos himenaeos.

Figure 7.18 Be sure to account for long labels in an effort to stress test your tab design.

Expanding Panels

Expanding panels (typically called *accordions*) come in many different shapes and sizes and are often lauded for their propensity to by touch-friendly (see **Figure 7.19**). You may find style inspiration (and consistency) from tabs, and vice versa. This is another benefit of designing the system instead of pages.

TOGGLE MENU ITEM 1
List Item one
List Item typewriter jean shorts high lifone
List Item three
List item number four
List Item five
elfies freegan wes anderson
gluten-free bushwick typewriter sriracha. Ethical
List Item seven elfies freegan wes
TOGGLE MENU ITEM 2
TOGGLE MENU ITEM 3

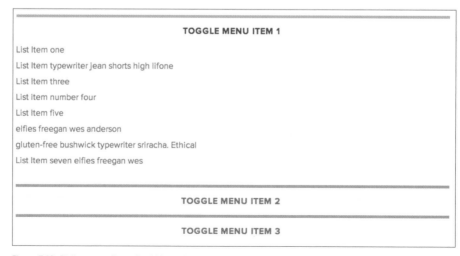

Figure 7.19 Styling accordions should be as fun as playing with them.

Comments

Comments typically take a format similar to media blocks, though they certainly don't have to do this. Depending on the amount of information you plan on showing, you may choose to float some left and right or stack everything vertically. It's good to work this out now or simply use a plug-in like Disqus.

Alerts

A fair amount of sites I've done have required an alert system (see **Figure 7.20**). A perfect example would be educational institutions, which require a large overlay that prohibits the user from engaging with the site until they acknowledge it or a small notification that rides along the top (most times it's both). I recommend inquiring about this component's inclusion in your project early on.

Figure 7.20 Alerts can include emergency notifications, system alerts, and error messages.

Latest/Recent Feeds

Lastly, almost every site has some type of listing component, where featured articles or latest news are pulled dynamically (see **Figure 7.21**). Besides feeds, you may be able to use similar styles for search results and calendar events. Defining some stylistic consistency over these components should be high priority.

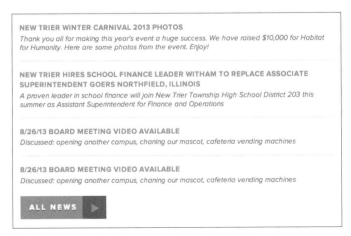

Figure 7.21 Feeds and results may warrant different styling than a default list of inline links.

Choosing the Best Environment for Your Components

Component libraries can be done in various levels of fidelity, but you're ultimately building a reference document for page development, so you'll want the final incarnation to be polished. Here's a look at the two environments you can produce them in.

HTML/CSS

As previously mentioned, my belief is that the style guide and component library should be done in production-ready code because the benefits are considerable. The browser provides the most flexible environment to test how responsive-friendly the components are, which is kind of a big deal, wouldn't you say? The browser is also the best place to assess any rendering or format issues from Safari to Internet Explorer. Above all, production-ready components are, well, ready for production and can be copied and pasted with ease, saving you time in the development of pages and templates.

Photoshop

So, why would anyone opt to build a component library in Photoshop? Depending on your code proficiency, team structure, or project, it may make sense to initially document components in Photoshop before moving them to the browser. I often find this suffers the same afflictions as page mock-ups do, in that you're duplicating the effort. However, you may find working in Photoshop for the purpose of ideation speeds up the process of the design happening in the browser.

Element collages can tell you a lot about the styles you want to deploy, but I've come to realize there's still a lot of figuring out to do at the component level. For those items I can't derive or interpret from the element collage, I hop back into Photoshop to resolve. It's still a bit arduous to re-create boxes and text and form fields, but Photoshop CC has made the job of consistency much easier for you, thanks to its new Libraries panel.

CC Libraries

Libraries have been one of the most requested Photoshop features over the years. You can imagine the ways being able to reuse assets would be beneficial to interface design in Photoshop; having to duplicate layers or re-create buttons is tedious. Thankfully, Creative Cloud (CC) Libraries aim to solve that pain point and many more.

While working within Photoshop, you can add any raster graphic, vector, or text to your Library (Window > Libraries) by dragging it over and dropping it on the panel. Your asset will be automatically categorized by type and ready to be reused in as many instances as you need.

Example: Creating a Button for Your Library

If this is your first go-round with CC Libraries, you might be confused about whether you can add only individual elements. The good news is that you can add complex elements easily. Let's try a button.

1. Open a new document, however big you want.

2. Create a rectangle. On a new layer, create text that says *button*.

3. Hold down the Shift key and select both the rectangle and text.

4. Release the Shift key and drag your complete button into the Libraries panel.

5. Drag your new asset back onto the canvas.

The Libraries panel respects the group you've dragged, even if it wasn't a linked layer or within a folder. The result, once dragged back to the canvas, is a fully editable button. How complex can you make it, you ask? You can even drag a Smart Object into Libraries and maintain its properties. Note that because it creates an new asset, don't expect any edits made on a new instance to carry through.

You can, however, add a Linked Smart Object to your Library and changes roll through.

Libraries are even more powerful cross-application (they're called "CC" Libraries for a reason). Often the logo and branding assets I receive from clients are in EPS format, which takes some copying and pasting to get into Photoshop. What's worse, those logos typically arrive in an email attachment that I rarely save locally, and when I do, it's in the bottomless pit called my Downloads folder. It's quite a pain when I need to use the logo again or if I'm the only one on my team with access to it.

CC Libraries can incorporate artwork from Illustrator and make it available to you in Photoshop, and vice versa. I believe this to be the original intent of the feature, though I rarely find myself going between applications, save the previous example. If you use Libraries for Photoshop only, you'll still get a lot use out of it.

Because CC Libraries are stored within your Creative Cloud account, they are easily shared with teammates you've allowed access to. Think of the possibilities for a moment. You could be working on one component in a Linked Smart Object while someone else works on another, only to have your components.psd update without anyone touching it. All of your shared assets in one place, finally.

Where's the latest version of the logo? Where can I find corporate green? Where's the obnoxious swoosh they're using in the print ads? All in our shared CC Library, of course. How silly of you thinking otherwise.

Lastly, I'd like to reiterate my opinion that Photoshop is super-helpful for the ideation of component styling, but the final execution should still take place in the browser, lest we lose the time we sought to gain. My hope is that you're able to create a style guide for content authors and a component library for developers, both documents doing more efficient legwork than that of the page mock-up.

Now that the Legos are defined, it's time to put them together.

Prototyping

Often missing in the comp-to-build process is the opportunity to test or to tweak as you collect input from the browser and your users. We get caught up in the craft of making things so precise in a static medium that they are often made to be exactly so in code.

In our effort to build a system, it'd be pretty difficult to jump to site completion from the pieces we've established. We have no assurance of how they'll mesh together on the page, from a functional flow and a visual one. That's where prototyping becomes the vehicle for page design (or for mid-to-large sites and templates).

A prototype may differ from a code-complete site in a few ways. Primarily, prototypes aren't backed by a CMS yet, since CMSs aren't always easy to adjust on the fly the way HTML & CSS are. We're moving toward a more finite build, but we want to keep the environment fairly flexible so we can pivot when we need to pivot. Our prototypes are still comprised of production-ready code (which is why it's important to use it in component-building), so we'll be ready to transition to the real deal with little re-engineering. If production-ready code isn't attainable, don't be discouraged; use code that shows your design intent and gets the job done so a developer can determine what needs refining.

Roughing It in Low-Fidelity

Do you need to wait until the element collage, style guide, and component library are all completed to start prototyping? Absolutely and positively not. In fact, preliminary sketches can fuel the prototype build around the time element collages are being explored. That's not to say you're working in polished high fidelity, but if you're proficient enough with HTML & CSS, you can explore some crude, gray-box mockups in the browser (see **Figure 7.22**). This is low-fidelity prototyping.

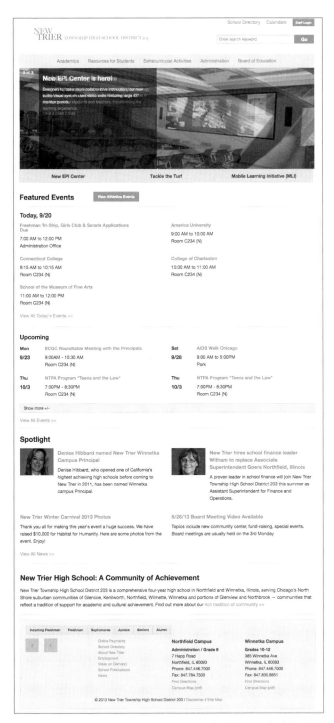

Figure 7.22 Gray boxes and blue links are a clear sign that no style choices have been made just yet, which keeps the focus on layout and content.

A rough idea of layout is a great place to start and gather inspiration for your components. I always like to pause and appreciate these moments where design and development can overlap and inform one another.

Getting Off the Ground with Low-Fidelity Prototype Frameworks

Perhaps you're a one-person shop or just looking to get in the browser but not completely confident you can pull off the tricks of a seasoned front-ender. A framework *may* be what you're looking for.

Zurb Foundation and Twitter Bootstrap are two of the finest and most reliable frameworks available. These kits will help you set up some gray-box prototypes in no time. Each comes packaged with the components I spoke of earlier in this chapter, as well as tons of documentation for implementation. I've used Foundation for years and love its ease of use.

Huge, major warning #1: You may be tempted to pass off these frameworks as production-ready code. While your templates may be succinct, I can guarantee you that there is a ton of CSS and JavaScript code you probably won't end up using (referred to as *bloat*). The goal of the framework is to give you everything you could possibly need, and stripping away what you don't isn't always easy.

Huge, major warning #2: There's a reason why Foundation sites look like Foundation sites and Bootstrap sites look like Bootstrap sites. The default buttons, typography, and layouts are great for low-fidelity prototyping but, if left unchanged, become identifiably commonplace high-fidelity styles. If you do continue using one of these frameworks, be sure to thoroughly purge any default style and consider any leftover details.

Most importantly, you want to be able to walk away from the low-fidelity prototypes feeling confident that everything works the way you intend it. Does the navigation have drop-down menus? Is there a fixed-position background? Does every element have an intentional adaptation across breakpoints? These are just some of the behaviors you want to be sure to nail, and stress test, before moving forward. You may find the ideas you toyed with in Photoshop have difficulty holding up across browser widths or with variable-length content.

Perhaps you work on a team with a developer who once inherited pixel-perfect mock-ups. If you're not comfortable learning a framework or writing code, prototyping is a great way to foster collaboration between the two of you. Because low-fidelity prototypes lack the style considerations you'd outline in your Photoshop comps, a simple sketch or working real-time with a developer to produce gray-box templates may be the most efficient methods for you.

High-Fidelity and Beyond!

I like to imagine the high-fidelity prototype as the culmination of style, function,and layout (see **Figure 7.23**). You explored style in the element collage, style guide, and component library. You explored function in the low-fidelity prototype. You explored facets of layout in everything you've done so far. You're ready.

Figure 7.23 All roads lead to the high-fidelity prototype, where style, layout, function, and content considerations meet.

If the low-fidelity prototype was done with production code, you'll have an easier time dropping in CSS from your style documents and seeing an immediate change to high-fidelity. If you used a framework as a stop-gap, a fair amount of markup edits stand between you and hi-fi glory.

Impressive. You've been able to use HTML & CSS for the bulk of your designing, heading back to Photoshop to toy with ideas. The best part is that you've created a consistent and reliable design system to build your site. Might as well close the book and call it a day, right?

Fortunately/unfortunately, establishing the system is only half the battle. Page and template design isn't automated from here, and you're about to see some of the ways responsive web design can throw a wrench into your work.

8

GETTING BACK INTO PHOTOSHOP WITH PAGE LAYERS

This is the first year my family is hosting Thanksgiving dinner. Although many people find it stressful to shoulder this responsibility, I love to cook, so I'm looking forward to it. I'm confident that I won't overcook the turkey. The texture of my mashed potatoes is always spot on. The rice recipe handed down to me from my grandmother has become my go-to dish to bring, so preparing and serving it on my home turf will make it even better. The cooking is going to go great.

It's the tablescape that has me petrified.

I know it sounds silly, but I don't quite know how to put everything together on the table—arguably, the most important part. Sure, you can say that it's all about how the food tastes, but if the food lacks presentation or is inaccessible, who's going to want to eat it? There's a lot of stuff to put out and not so much space to put it in, let alone make it look elegant.

Fortunately, my family is comfortable retrieving their own utensils should I forget to give them any, just as they're sure to trade seats until everyone is in closest proximity to their favorite dishes.

As designers, we don't have the convenience of knowing our users will willingly adapt to our designs. How we design the page can make or break the experience. *Does the arrangement make sense? Does each element look intentional? Does this look like a cohesive page?*

We have all the dishes, but the table will look like a hot mess without a game plan.

Rough Waters Ahead

In the world of RWD, the potential number of layouts we need to consider can be overwhelming at times. Screens are small, wide, tall, short, or the middle of all the above. When we throw components at a page, our expectation is that everything will just magically pop into place. I mean, everything has a consistent style and is responsively built, so what's the worst that can happen?

The answer is, a white page with a bunch of awkwardly distributed content (see **Figure 8.1**).

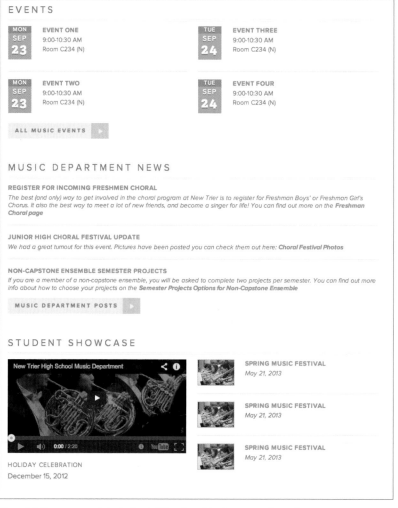

Figure 8.1 The components look nice, but there's nothing to group or frame them.

To break it down further, there are usually four problems I find myself wrestling with after I port components into page templates.

▶ It's a struggle to increase fidelity.

▶ There's no easy way to suggest tweaks.

▶ The pages lack cohesion.

▶ Some elements suffer from responsive wonkiness.

This chapter will address those challenges in detail because it's not until we resolve these issues that we can deliver well-considered designs. The good news is that each struggle can benefit from a little bit of TLC in Photoshop. What complicates matters is that everything we have, from style guides to component libraries, is in code. How do we get the product of HTML & CSS back into Photoshop?

The solution may blow your mind.

Introducing Page Layers

Every attempt I've made to go from rendered web page to Photoshop has been an exercise in futility. I just end up re-creating every shape, entering each line of text, and ultimately banging my head on my desk for the time it took to do so. Thankfully, there's a better way and it's called Page Layers.

Created by Ralf Ebert, Page Layers (see **Figure 8.2**) is a Mac app that converts HTML to PSD. The presentation of the app is akin to a browser, with only a few differences. To export a page, type in the URL, and when the page loads, choose Screenshot > Save As or drag the PSD icon at the top right to your folder of choice. Page Layers will parse through the page and create a PSD with layers respective to the DOM, or structure of the HTML. The result is a perfectly captured web page that's fully editable, layer by layer, in Photoshop.

It's magic, really. For $34.99 (on the Mac App Store), it's also a bargain. If you're unimpressed at this point, I'm confident I'll convert you to Team Page Layers by demonstrating how it helps solve our four component-to-page problems.

Figure 8.2 Page Layers (*www.pagelayers.com*) is a magical application that turns your website into a fully layered Photoshop document.

The Struggle to Increase Fidelity

As you move toward creating a high-fidelity prototype, you'll encounter a few scenarios where you're likely to struggle with bringing the right amount of polish to your design. Perhaps you're still designing components and you're stuck on how to style a few. Maybe you'll encounter a block of content that isn't a repeatable pattern so much as it's a page-specific occurrence. For many of us, the process of refining components can lead into the trap of attempting to design everything in the browser.

As mentioned in Chapter 4, designing in the browser can often yield results that align with the path of least resistance. Boxes, solid colors, and habitual styling, even unintentionally applied, can prove counterproductive in some projects. You might hit a creative wall when you're trying to style components, such as footers, that don't inherently lend themselves to the design inspiration captured in the visual inventory or element collage. In many a project I've found the gray-boxed footer staring me in the eye, challenging me to come up with something beyond my usual solid background color overlaid by white text links.

This is where Page Layers shines. Instead of trying to vet ideas in the browser, fire up Page Layers and export the component you're struggling with back into Photoshop. It may be the most fundamental use case for Page Layers, but using it as a means to retrieve usable assets in Photoshop is undeniably essential.

With full-page comps, in cases where we needed to edit something, we always had an original we could start from. If we ditch this approach, Page Layers becomes indispensable as a tool to give us access to every page element in Photoshop. Quite simply, we now have the best starting point to begin high-fidelity ideation.

Let's start with the example of a low-fidelity prototype. It's strewn with gray boxes and unstyled text, by design. When it's time to move to component styling and you're struggling to add fidelity to the footer, there's no need to hop into Photoshop and attempt to re-create all the links. Fire up Page Layers, generate a PSD of your lo-fi, and use the time you would have re-creating elements to build your dream footer instead (see **Figure 8.3**).

TIP Page Layers renders elements as raster graphics, making it a little tricky to manipulate them. While a fix for vector rendering is ideally in the works, you can render text for easy editing by choosing Save As instead of dragging the PSD icon. In the dialog that appears, select the Generate Text Layers check box. It's likely the name of the web font being used won't map to any installed on your computer, so you'll need to adjust it manually.

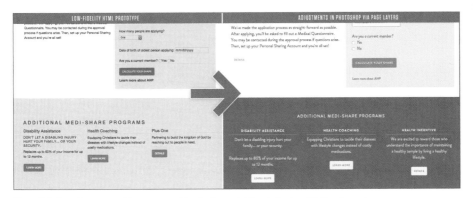

Figure 8.3 Page Layers provides a reasonable starting point for styling low-fidelity elements.

Pulling your rough layouts into Photoshop is a great way to start adjusting in an environment of direct manipulation, and it may increase your efficiency in homing in on the best stylistic approach.

Don't Get *Too* Comfortable in Photoshop

The first few times I used Page Layers were game-changing. It was so game-changing, in fact, that I found myself spending too much time in Photoshop and not getting back into the browser to implement my ideas. It's surprisingly easy, and addictive, to start pulling in page after page and adjust every last detail. The problem is that method isn't much better than creating full-page comps prior to development.

Try to focus on only those components or areas that could use a quick round of ideation. If you find yourself (or your team) spending more time in Photoshop than coding, that's not the balance we're looking for. Our goal is to use Photoshop as a complement to the browser, not an equal or superior. Keeping this in mind should help you move between the two environments with frequency and efficiency. Continue to rely on the visual inventory and element collage where you can; where you can't, move quickly through your ideas in Photoshop.

Leveraging Linked Smart Objects

Linked Smart Objects are one of the best features in Photoshop CC. If you're unfamiliar with Smart Objects in general, they are layers in your document that contain nested elements. For example, you may have a component such as navigation in a Smart Object. The individual type layers or shapes that comprise it wouldn't appear in your parent PSD; rather, they'd be isolated in a child PSD, accessed by double-clicking the layer thumbnail.

For years, to edit those Smart Objects, you would need to have the parent PSD open. With Linked Smart Objects, child PSBs can remain independent files from the parent but still update the parent when saved. It's a feature similar to Links in InDesign, where any changes made to exterior files are reflected in the parent INDD.

So, what does this mean for component-driven design? If you're a solo designer, Linked Smart Objects might provide a decent way to organize your ideas.

More importantly, if you're on a team of designers, Linked Smart Objects resolve the conflict of any two designers needing to make changes to the same PSD simultaneously. In this example, components.psd is a master document comprised only of Linked Smart Objects. Kenny Loggins can be editing header.psb while Jim Messina edits carousel.psb (see **Figure 8.4**). This gives Loggins complete autonomy over a portion of the master PSD without needing to ask Messina for permission to edit it.

If this workflow sounds appealing to you and your team, you might consider the following workspace beneficial. In one window, you can edit a component and in another window view components.psd updating live.

Linked Smart Objects offer a powerful way to get multiple designers working on the same part of the process simultaneously, which again should help productivity and efficiency.

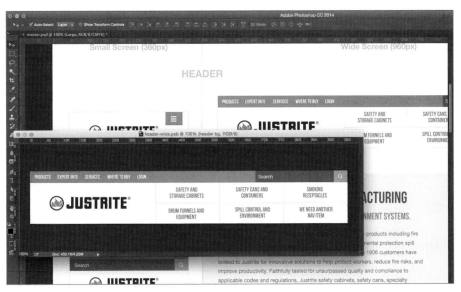

Figure 8.4 Here's Loggins working on the header on the left. His changes are reflected in the master PSD on the right, without ever needing to touch it.

There's No Easy Way to Suggest Tweaks

No matter your level of experience, I wager you can identify with this common practice:

1. You notice something in development that needs adjusting.

2. You take a screen grab and pull it into Photoshop.

3. You adjust the offending element through a mix of clone stamping, re-creating text, and other smoke-and-mirrors approaches.

The Old Screenshot

No doubt, we designers have gotten good at this practice, even when it's just to make a suggestion to another designer instead of trying to describe it with words. Pictures do a much better and more accurate job, so why not lean on our proficiency in Photoshop to tell the story? My team at WSOL does this constantly over Slack (an instant messaging communication tool I highly recommend). As efficient as I thought I was at this method of picture making, it still takes me 10 to 20 minutes at times to produce a comp with stretched-out text and gaps in the background (see **Figure 8.5**).

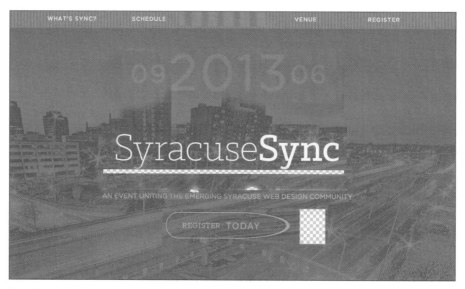

Figure 8.5 The modifications of this screenshot are less than desirable, wouldn't you say?

Fellow designers can usually interpret such deformities, but it's less than ideal to hand this to a developer. It usually takes more explaining than it should. What's worse is attempting to modify a screen grab to illustrate a point to your clients. It'd be best to not have to disclaimer your work.

The New Screenshot

Thankfully, we don't have to. With Page Layers, we have all the assets at the ready for transforming and editing. Because every element is on its own layer, there's no need for filling in patches where you selected a region and moved it or stretching or squishing text to fit a new container. The ease with which we can modify these "screenshots" has significant impact on our accuracy and efficiency. Let's take a look at three benefits.

A Proper Sandbox

For code-averse designers, suggesting adjustments in Photoshop has always been the best option. It's a familiar environment in which we can maintain the fidelity of the browser. Even for the designer who codes but is fearful of any ripple effect their efforts may cause to development (raises hand), Photoshop provides a sterile environment in which major adjustments have no repercussions. I consider myself proficient in HTML & CSS, but I find myself making small pictures for our front-end developer, who's at least twice as efficient as I am.

Using Smarter Guides

Predictably, the PSD you capture from Page Layers doesn't come with any guides. While that's not devastating, it's often helpful to have something to align to when you're comping. Thankfully, features like New Guides and Smart Guides are just what you need. Here's how to use them:

New Guides

1. To add a New Guide at a specific pixel value, choose View > New Guide.

2. To add a set or grid of New Guides, choose View > New Guide Layout. In the dialog that opens, you can set the rows, columns, and amount of guides (remember to check Preview to get a sneak peek before committing).

3. To add New Guides based on the edges of an element, select its layer and choose View > New Guides from Shape. Even if it's not a vector shape, Photoshop will draw guides that align to the vertical and horizontal edges of the element. This is super-handy for alignment of new assets.

Smart Guides

1. Make sure Smart Guides (View > Show > Smart Guides) and Rulers (View > Rulers) are turned on.

2. Hold Option/Alt and drag a layer to duplicate the element. As you're dragging, notice the pink guides indicating the distance from the original, as well as alignment guides to snap to.

3. Press Command/Ctrl and hover over an element to display similar guides and information.

Cumulative Time Savings

You may snicker at the concept of saving time with more efficient doodling in Photoshop. A 20-minute exercise is reduced by half in Page Layers, but 10 minutes isn't going to help us come in under budget any more than 20 might. While that may be true, consider the cumulative time savings of 10 minutes here, 10 minutes there. This practice of modifying screenshots is so commonplace for most teams that they can find themselves saving hours with this adjustment.

Maybe it's not about budget for you. Still, imagine having a conversation with a developer about a page when you notice something that can change. If it takes you 20 minutes to communicate the necessary adjustment, that's 20 minutes they've been waiting for your response or potentially have moved onto something else. Quicker adjustments through Page Layers help to sustain the momentum of the conversation and potentially help you figure out what you want to suggest a lot faster, too.

Reinforcing the Practice

Using visual aides to communicate our design recommendations seems natural, right? We continue to modify screenshots because we know the power of being able to show our intent visually, complementing our words. Sometimes I tend to lose sight of this, because the mere thought of hacking a screenshot in Photoshop seems like more trouble than it's worth. Regretfully, this has resulted in more utterances of "that looks good enough" than I'm comfortable admitting.

For me, Page Layers has made an arduous task easier, so much so that I tend to use it more often. It's hard to argue against anything that helps you communicate design intent more efficiently.

Our Pages Lack Cohesion

Designing a system has major advantages over page-centric design, especially in responsive contexts. I've hinted at some of these benefits already: increased consistency, thoroughness, and modularity. I know I need a button on the page, but instead of creating a one-off style for it, I refer to the style guide. This is a good approach; embrace it.

However, when we move to building out pages and templates, the premise that we can just plop in our components and everything should look intentional is a bit misguided. We've established some stylistic consistency across each component, but that doesn't guarantee their arrangement on a page will look well considered. I believe a lot of the similarities found across responsive sites are because of a lack of page cohesion and a reliance on designing in the browser.

Framing Content and the Big Picture

In Chapter 4, I touched on a theme called *responsive design sameness*. Sites today are just one level of consideration shy of establishing more of a unique identity. Let's break this down a bit further.

On a site I created for Indiana Wesleyan University, I added a few components to the middle of the homepage. At the very least, everything is where it needs to be, but like so many other sites, we have a bunch of content floating atop a white background. Is it functional? Yes. Is it legible? Yes. Is it cohesive? I'd argue that it's not, at least not with the other content above and below it. It lacks character and presentation (see **Figure 8.6**).

Figure 8.6 On their own, the components make for a totally usable design, but the content isn't framed in any meaningful way.

With Page Layers, I took this back to Photoshop to toy with some ideas I had to better frame the About Us content. In the context of a large photographic banner on top and a footer below whose background is a campus photo, introducing a third, more subtle photo seemed natural. I find it a thousand times easier to manipulate photos and effects in Photoshop than in the browser and thus have the propensity to do so more often. What resulted after a round or two was a clearly defined panel for the content and, more importantly, an opportunity to help introduce some cohesive style to a section that desperately needed it (see **Figure 8.7**).

Figure 8.7 Much better. Photography goes a long way in bringing your audience into an environment.

It's worth noting that one of the best techniques for repurposing Photoshop isn't focusing on the pixel-level detail we're accustomed to but the broad canvas of the page. If we can borrow a step from the traditional process, the ability to step back (zoom out, rather) and view the entire page was a very underrated byproduct of the granular work we were doing. Designing in the browser tends to lock us into a viewport's height, making it harder to assess cohesiveness and flow across the entire page. Worse yet, how easy is it to design solely for the particular height of your browser window, only to realize that your design doesn't work at a different height?

Bird's-Eye View

Living in a house that's barely a year old, I've started to become enamored with yard work. Early on, after growing an acre's worth of grass (which was no small feat, mind you), I decided to take on some landscaping. My wife and I made our way down to a local nursery and bought nine small plants, and I spent the better part of a few weekends making some beds for them to grow in. I'm happy with the result, though it wasn't until recently that I saw our house on Google Earth and noticed how isolated everything looks in view of our entire lot. We have a swing set here, two small apple trees there, and a bed of plants near neither.

I'm glad I had an aerial view at this point. It's spurred tons of ideas for planting large trees, how big to make a patio, and what size pool would work (just kidding—people in Syracuse don't have pools). While it's not realistic that my house will be viewed from that perspective, I do know that being too close to the "component" I'm working on tends to lend itself to looking isolated in view of the big picture.

Sometimes, Photoshop is better used as Google Earth than Street View.

Where Skeuomorphism Worked

Cohesiveness is one of page design's toughest challenges; in this regard, it trails only establishing layout and hierarchy. It would seem that our fixed-width—dare I say skeuomorphic—designs took cohesion into account more than our responsive, flat-designed sites. With the more detailed, textural designs, we had to take great consideration as to deep layering of backgrounds, transitions of content sections, and how we established clarity (see **Figure 8.8**). Minimal, flat-design aesthetics are convenient for responsive design since there is a fair amount of margin of error in terms of our backgrounds adapting to different widths. With that, I fear we haven't always considered the details of stitching components together in a deliberate way.

Figure 8.8 It's often difficult to make sections of solid colors seem cohesive.

I'm not advocating for employing a bunch of one-off section backgrounds; such faulty logic will catch up to you as you try to maintain a handful of slightly different section styles. Introducing a better way to frame content in one place should be applicable to other places on your site. Alternatively, push yourself to find more methods than employing solid background colors with hard edges; there's plenty of that out there already. Instead, elements such as rules, padding, and even gradients may give you more distinctive solutions.

Some Elements Suffer from Responsive Wonkiness

Let's talk about being responsively thorough for a minute. If we're adopting the philosophy that our site should look its best at *any* size, that means we need to test it beyond the most popular or convenient-to-us device widths. Resizing our browser gives us a decent approximation, but if that's the route we're taking, I encourage you to set it to something peculiar like 734px. If you're like me, you'll find the 50px above or below a breakpoint are certain to produce some kind of oddities.

I like to define "oddities" as anything that looks wonky and "wonkiness" as a presentation that isn't quite ideal. For instance, the three circles shown here are adequately filled at 900px, and though the content is abbreviated, it's still optimal at 800px. However, the circles begin to have some undesirable empty space at 850px. Granted, you may not have a large user base viewing your site on a 850px device, but it's certainly possible someone's browser window is open that wide at any given time. Any way you rationalize it, I think you need to take another look at this component's 850px presentation (see **Figure 8.9**).

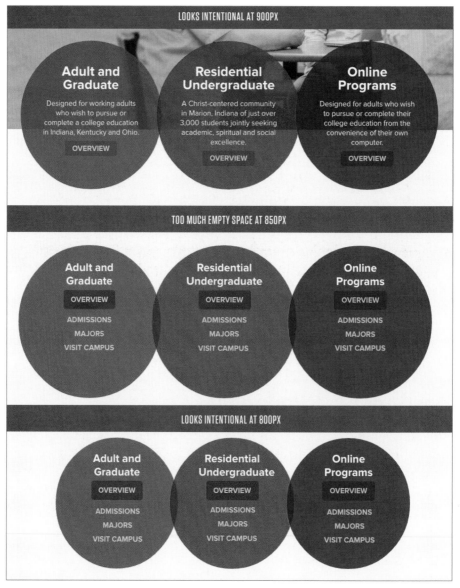

Figure 8.9 The content fills the circles well at 800px and 900px but not so much at 850px. I contend that's worth fixing.

Seems pretty particular, no? I enjoy this take on the matter:

“Go deeper. Squander loose time on expanding your ideas, even if you're sure they're perfect or useless. Look closely at decisions you think are trivial. I guarantee you'll find better solutions around the corner.”

—CENNYD BOWLES, Letter to a Junior Designer (*www.alistapart.com/column/ letter-to-a-junior-designer*)

Examples like this provide opportunities to really nail the interface across the board. Do you need to make changes to the entire site at 850px? Not at all. You can add as many component-specific breakpoints as you need to respond to the stress, or stretch, of your designs (see **Figure 8.10**).

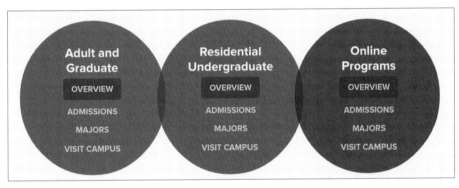

Figure 8.10 A tiny media query whose sole purpose is addressing the circle space and nothing more

Width-Specificity in Page Layers

Identifying wonkiness is one thing. Fixing it is another matter. Again, Page Layers can help us take a screenshot back into Photoshop for some ideation (see **Figure 8.11**). Because it acts like a browser, the Page Layers application can be resized to the exact width of your responsive oddity; then it can capture a representative PSD. What's more, you can find the exact dimensions on the top left of the app, which will be handy for recalling which value you need a breakpoint at.

Figure 8.11 Page Layers provides live dimensions of your browser window.

All in all, Page Layers is an indispensable application if you want to address RWD with Photoshop. I suppose the fact that it's a Mac-only product is a bit of a bummer. The live text capture incompatibilities and lack of vectorizing shapes are a little disheartening, but the benefits far outweigh these conveniences. I've saved countless hours and frustration being able to get back into an environment I can vet ideas and creativity greater than a code editor.

(If Adobe wants to someone incorporate this function into Photoshop natively or a similar companion app so it's accessible cross-platform, I imagine a lot of people would be happy.)

Exit Strategy

Let's briefly recap what we've been able to accomplish in Photoshop. We've added fidelity to some gray-box prototypes. Our screenshot modifications potentially have some new elements we've shown to our developers. We've added some backgrounds and frames to otherwise floating content. We've even suggested alternatives to those pesky in-between breakpoint oddities.

It sounds to me like we have a handful of Photoshop assets we need to implement in the browser—if only there were an easier way than the arduous Save for Web.

Would you believe the cropping, slicing, and Mac OS X beach ball-inducing workflow isn't our only option? The efficiency train is moving full steam ahead, and exporting our assets just bought us a ticket.

9

EXTRACTING YOUR WAY
OUT OF PHOTOSHOP

My hope is that Page Layers, explored in Chapter 8, gives you a reasonable way to go from the browser to Photoshop. Now you can turn your attention to the opposite: taking all the assets you've created or adjusted in Photoshop and bringing them back out to the browser.

Prior to Photoshop CC, the options weren't great. Anything beyond a simple CSS tweak posed a challenge, especially if it involved exporting an image. How many times have you saved a PNG only to find out there's a hairline or two of built-in padding throwing off its positioning? Worse yet are the times you forgot to turn off a layer that makes its way into your exported graphic.

Efficiently extracting assets from Photoshop is crucial to an RWD workflow. If you stumble here, it's bound to cost you considerable time you could spend doing something else. The whole point of getting back into Photoshop is to refine your ideas quicker than you can in code. If the process of getting out of Photoshop nullifies the time spent in it, you might as well have never gone back in the first place.

Thankfully, this chapter demonstrates how Photoshop CC is built to help you save significant time in this area. To fully understand how, and why, let's take a look at the previous set of options.

Asset Extraction Is Like Pulling Teeth

"Pulling teeth" is just about the best analogy I can make for saving out images or useful information from Photoshop. Unfortunately, the pain isn't exclusive to the exporter (you) but shared with the lucky individual who inherits your work (your developer, if it's not you as well). Every method, hacky or otherwise, has its share of inefficiencies, as described in the following sections.

Crop and Save

The most apparent way to churn out images from Photoshop, and one I adopted for many years, was to crop around each item individually and save it as an image (JPEG or PNG).

If there's only one asset to export, this isn't a terrible method. It's quick and relatively easy to do. It's only when there are multiple assets to crop that the process becomes arduous. Still, some designers prefer the amount of control they have over defining the bounds of the crop on a case-by-case basis.

Speaking of the crop, I find it incredibly difficult to consistently match the edges of my asset. For example, the icons shown in **Figure 9.1** have no square edges to align to. I did a decent job of making the last two snug, but you can see that the first exported image has a hairline of extra space to the left, which drives my developer nuts trying to align it with the others.

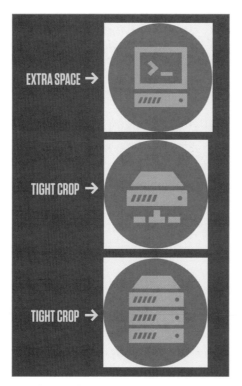

Figure 9.1 Drat. That throws off the spacing a bit, doesn't it?

On closer inspection, there's a barely visible blue background behind the icons (see **Figure 9.2**). I must have forgotten to turn off that layer. No problem; I'll just go back and re-crop everything all over again. There's no better use of my time, I'm sure.

The king of this comedy of errors is the Save function. Save in Photoshop will return an uncompressed version of your work. I've just made these tiny icons 100KB each (see **Figure 9.3**). Ouch. Now for the *piece de resistance*: mistakenly saving the cropped artwork as my PSD and closing the document, only to find out when I re-open it that everything is lost. Double ouch. Infinity ouch, even.

Figure 9.2 Icons with and without the faint blue background layer that should have been turned off. Whoops.

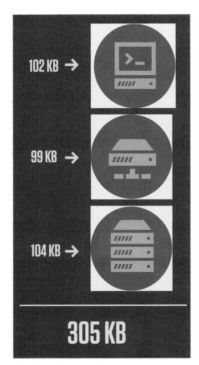

Figure 9.3 It's probably not within my performance budget to have three icons amass 300KB.

Why File Size Matters

It's arguable that website speed and performance have never been more important than they are today. Only briefly could you assume that your audience was sitting at a desktop, albeit rarely with a high-speed Internet connection. In those cases, 3MB images rendered instantly on the page, 10MB pages rendered in a second or two, and we didn't need to be all too particular about optimizing file size.

Although some mobile networks are growing increasingly faster, 10MB over cellular data is a considerable amount to download and render. According to Verizon Wireless, a 10MB transfer on a 2G network could take upward of 16 minutes (*www.verizonwireless.com/news/article/2014/05/a-day-in-the-life-with-2g-speed.html*).

Worse yet, mobile subscribers are charged for roaming or going over their data plans. Andy Clarke noted the following in regard to viewing the 85MB monstrosity that was *http://moto.oakley.com*: "If you were data roaming on an iPhone, at $9 per megabit data roaming, that web page would cost me $785 to look at on my iPhone!"

If you don't optimize your images for speed's sake, do it for everyone's wallets. While you're at it, do it for everyone stuck on a slow connection at Panera, the car repair shop, and their distant relative's vacation house too.

Copy Merged

Copy Merged (see **Figure 9.4**) is a technique similar to cropping, with an added twist. Draw a rectangular marquee around the graphic you want, choose Edit > Copy Merged (Command/Ctrl+Shift+C), and then paste it into a new document by choosing File > New. The primary advantage this approach has over cropping is not having to worry about saving a cropped PSD. Otherwise, it still suffers from the afflictions of mis-cropping (technically, mis-selecting) and tediousness across multiple assets.

Figure 9.4 Many designers have adopted Copy Merged as the best method to exact assets.

Save for Web

If you listen closely, right now, you can hear the sound of someone's Photoshop crashing. The moment you choose Save for Web and see the beach ball of death in Mac OS X (see **Figure 9.5**), so many thoughts run through your head. *When was the last time I saved this? Did I ever save this? Maybe I'll just leave Photoshop to process this for a while and come back later.*

Figure 9.5 Scream in terror as the dreaded beach ball of death draws nigh.

I'm not sure why, but historically, Save for Web has always given Photoshop a performance problem. While I can't say reliably that Photoshop CC has addressed this, there are other drawbacks to using the feature. Unless you want to roll with the cropping or Copy Merged method, slicing is your best bet for a Save for Web workflow (see **Figure 9.6**). I'm not sure about you, but I've never been able to get slices exactly where I want them. They always snap to the edge of a different element or end up one pixel off.

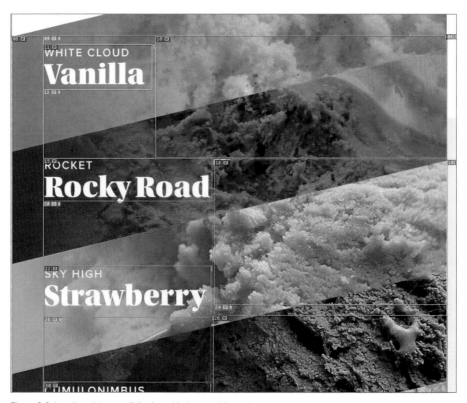

Figure 9.6 I can't wait to see all the 1px-wide images this produces.

At best, setting up slices makes for more effort than I'm willing to spend. Save for Web will helpfully compress your assets, but it's not the fastest workflow to employ.

We need a lightning-quick way to get this stuff out of Photoshop, not one that relies on our ability to align rules, guides, and selections.

Adobe Generator

The addition of Adobe Generator in Photoshop CC will save you pain and valuable time. Generator is an engine built into Photoshop that's capable of extracting assets in real time. Here's the easiest example of its use:

1. Append any layer name with a file extension, such as sample.jpg or sample.png.

2. Choose File > Generate > Image Assets.

   A folder with your PSD's name and the suffix "-assets" will appear in the directory where your PSD lives, full of any files you've specified as layer names.

Generator has provided an immediate alternative, and improvement, to the aforementioned extraction methods and should give the efficiency you need in getting back to the browser. Let's break down how it works and how to get the most out of it.

Auto-magic Generation

The first time I used Generator, its real-time generation of image assets blew me away. Saving your PSD isn't required; any change you make to a layer that has a file extension in its layer name is immediately reflected in the exported file. Because this updating is happening in the background, you can continue to focus your attention on editing your artwork in Photoshop without having to stop and complete export settings each time you want an asset.

This is a fairly radical concept compared to traditional workflows, which hinged on refining all of your work prior to exporting everything at once. Once the Generator switch is on, it'll continue to monitor your layers and pump out assets or edits to those assets until you switch it off (see **Figure 9.7**).

Figure 9.7 Abracadabra! Your images are waiting for you in the background.

This feature has its greatest potential if your assets are being generated to a development folder. As soon as an icon is changed in Photoshop, it's reflected on the Web. That kind of relationship between Photoshop and the browser didn't exist before Adobe introduced Generator. Some designer may opt for a layer of control between generated assets and a live or development site simply because automatically overwriting files can be kind of scary. Nevertheless, it's exciting to see this line of communication opened.

Pixel Precision

Upon first use, I still had some skepticism about relying on Generator. How trustworthy was it? The test it needed to pass was one of precision. My assumption was that the images it exported were rough estimates of their bounds, meaning that there'd be some unwanted empty space baked in. To my surprise, assets are cropped to their exact edges, with not one pixel of padding (see **Figure 9.8**). Phew.

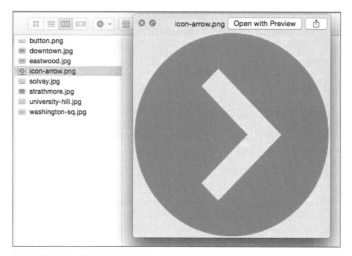

Figure 9.8 Beautifully cropped

Welcome to the party, Generator.

Speaking Fluent Generator

Generator can be basic or advanced, depending on your needs. Let's take a look at each file format it can produce and its options.

JPEG

TIP Generator compresses assets using an open source utility called ImageMagick, independent of the compression methods of Save As or Save for Web. It's helpful to make this distinction in case you're wondering why the quality values aren't 1–12 like they are in Save As.

By default, a layer named "sample.jpg" will export as a compressed JPEG at 90 percent quality. Should you prefer a different quality setting, naming your layer "sample.jpg10%" will export a JPEG at 10 percent quality, naming it "sample.jpg20%" will export at 20 percent quality, and so on. You can also use quality values of 1–10, such as sample.jpg5, sample.jpg6, and so on.

PNG

Tagging a layer with .png will generate a PNG 32 with alpha transparency by default. If you desire a PNG 24, name your layer "sample.png24," or for a PNG 8, name it "sample.png8."

GIF

You can also generate GIFs from Photoshop by tagging your layer "sample.gif." There aren't any compression options to set, and Generator will export with alpha transparency.

SVG

If you're a practitioner of RWD, Scalable Vector Graphics (SVGs) should be your new BFF.

Whereas JPEG and PNG images are bound to the dimensions they're exported as, SVGs can scale to their Hypertext Markup Language (HTML) container independent of the size they were created at (see **Figure 9.9**). That's because SVG is a format based on Extensible Markup Language (XML) that draws the shape in the browser.

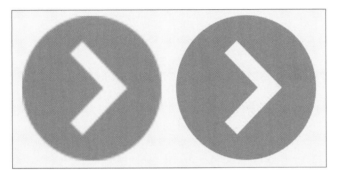

Figure 9.9 Two images scaled up in the browser: a PNG (left) and an SVG (right)

Using SVG to Change Color

One major advantage of using SVGs is the ability to manipulate color dynamically with CSS. Instead of exporting separate images for a default state and a hover state of an image (think: icons), CSS can change the fill when necessary (see **Figure 9.10**).

Figure 9.10 The hover state is being controlled by CSS, not a separate image or background position.

Multiple Formats

Producing a fallback PNG for an SVG is a one-step process with Generator, a major advantage over multistep processes in Illustrator or other programs. Here's an example of a single layer name that will produce multiple files:

"sample.svg, sample.png"

Simple, right? You can even replace the comma with a plus sign (+), should you so desire.

Sizes

Let's take that a bit further. For non-SVG assets that you'd like to scale for high-density displays such as Apple's Retina screens, you'll need to be able to increase or decrease the size of your artwork in Photoshop accordingly. Again, Generator makes this a cakewalk.

"sample.jpg, 200% sample.jpg"

This will produce two JPGs, one double the size of the other. Producing assets for high-density displays does take some consideration before you start building artwork. For instance, doubling the size of a raster image like a photograph will produce blurry results. Instead, starting with a photograph fit for Retina screens and reducing it by half should give you proper images for both screens.

"sample.jpg, 50% sample.jpg"

Here are two last notes on sizing your images with Generator: Multiple formats are allowed ("sample.jpg, sample.png"), as well as sizing files by dimension rather than percentage ("300x300 sample.png"). Dimensions will default to pixels, but you can specify having them rendered as in, cm, or mm for inches, centimeters, or millimeters, respectively.

Groups

If you want to get really fancy, place a file extension on a group folder in Photoshop. The result? One merged asset of the contents of the group. This is especially useful for photo manipulations strewn across multiple layers.

Exporting to Folders

It's possible you wouldn't want to dump all your assets in the same folder. At WSOL, we separate our images by use: We have a "content" folder for any images intended to be uploaded through the CMS and a "ui" folder for any images that are part of the templates. Instead of sorting through your generated assets folder, leverage the power of Generator to do the job for you.

"content/photo.jpg" places photo.jpg inside the folder named "content."

"ui/icon-star.png" places icon-star.png inside the folder named "ui."

Generator also supports subfolders, should you want to be extra-organized.

Layer Naming as a Practice

A counterpoint to the convenience of Generator often comes from designers who don't name their layers in the first place. Essentially, are you saving any more time having to name all your layers in the end than selecting each layer and Save for Web?

Your time savings are most likely minimal, at best.

That's where the beauty of Generator is for me. If you name your layers *as you go*, you can experience significant time savings. Generator, albeit indirectly, advocates for better organization on the part of the designer. I'll discuss the benefits of such "etiquette" in Chapter 11, but naming your layers as you create them has a direct impact on how efficient the Generator workflow can be.

Beyond organization, Generator also goes hand in hand with naming your layers accurately. Generic layer names like "button" or "Shape" don't make for easy filenames to employ on your site. What kind of button? What function does the shape have? Instead, thinking in terms of filenames will help identify their use in development. I much prefer "button-primary.png" over "button.png" and prefer "icon-arrow.png" over "Shape.png."

Adobe Generator is clearly a powerful tool for speeding up your workflow. I've covered only the current Photoshop manifestation of it, image assets. Some of third-party services I'll cover in Chapter 10 leverage it in unique ways as well. The future is bright for this feature, especially if it can continue to build on the communication between Photoshop and the browser.

Extract Assets

If you like the concept of Generator, you'll love a new feature called Extract Assets. Essentially a UI layer on top of Generator, Extract Assets provides a dialog to choose all of the convenient options I've just discussed (see **Figure 9.11**). You can choose to extract assets a layer at a time or add a group's entire contents to be generated.

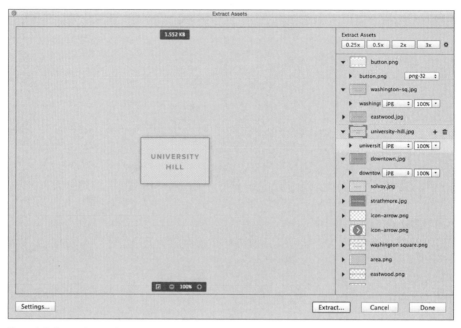

Figure 9.11 Extract Assets, Generator's UI

Extract Assets will rename your layers with the Generator syntax for you. That means that whenever you change a tagged layer's appearance, it will be automatically reflected in the generated file.

If automatically generated assets don't sound appealing to you, in the lower left of the Extract Assets dialog, click Settings, and deselect the "Automatically generate assets when updating document" check box.

Setup

You'll find the Extract Assets menu by choosing File > Extract Assets or by selecting one or multiple layers, right-clicking in the Layers panel, and choosing Extract Assets. If no layers are selected or tagged when you choose Extract Assets from the File menu, you'll be prompted to select a layer before proceeding. Via keyboard shortcut, it's Cmd+Option+Shift+W (Mac OS) or Ctrl+Alt+Shift+W (Windows).

The dialog has a similar appearance to Save for Web, showing a preview of the selected layer on the left and an options panel on the right. Now that you have an eye on minimizing file size through image optimization, pay attention to the value just above the image preview; it's a live preview of the expected file size (see **Figure 9.12**).

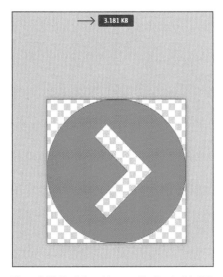

Figure 9.12 Don't forget to pay attention to this little guy.

The options start with Asset Resolution presets of 0.25x, 0.5x, 2x, and 3x. For greater control over the sizes, suffixes, and folder names of additional resolutions, choose Settings in the lower left.

TIP Didn't name your layer something filename-friendly to begin with? No worries—you can rename it from within the Extract Assets dialog.

If you're like me, you'll select a bunch of layers and select Extract Assets only to realize you're missing one. Fortunately, Photoshop makes it easy to keep the dialog open and select the missing one from the Layers panel. As soon as you do, you'll see a message in the lower right of the Extract Assets dialog that says "Add Assets for 'Your-Layer-Name'?" Choose Add, and you're all set (see **Figure 9.13**).

Extract Assets provides a friendly interface for those familiar and, more importantly, unfamiliar with Generator. Developers can go into your comp or element collage to grab any necessary images. The only assumption you make here is that your developer has a copy of Photoshop too.

But what if they don't?

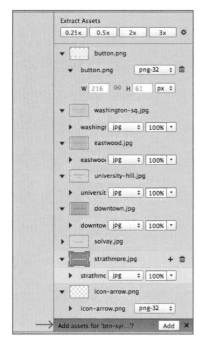

Figure 9.13 Phew. Adding in a missing layer is convenient.

Extract

Think for a moment about the types of things you or someone you work with needs from a PSD. Typically, it has little to do with specific layout. You're looking to grab small images, color values, and font settings. Even if you do have Photoshop, it's not always convenient to open it just to procure this kind of information.

I'm happy to report there is an alternative, and it's called Extract.

Integrated into Creative Cloud, Extract is an online service that reads the content of a PSD *sans* Photoshop. All someone needs to use it is a Creative Cloud account, even a free one. Let's take a look at extracting the most out of the service. (See what I did there? OK, I'll stop.)

Setup

To start using Extract, go to your Creative Cloud profile by signing into Adobe.com. Under Assets, select Files. Choose an existing PSD or upload one by choosing Actions > Upload. By default, the next screen you'll see is Extract view (see **Figure 9.14**).

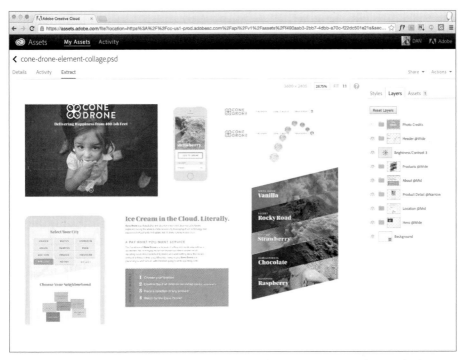

Figure 9.14 Extract lives in the browser and is free to all Creative Cloud members, making for easy adoption among teams.

The left portion of the app shows the PSD, while the right holds all the valuable information worth extracting. Choosing a layer, or multiple layers, in the PSD updates the information on the right. Simultaneously, a blue box with quick actions such as Copy CSS or Download will appear upon choosing a layer.

Downloading Assets via Libraries

TIP You can combine multiple elements into one image by holding Shift and selecting them first and then pressing the download arrow.

Extracting images is a straightforward but involved process in Extract. Start by selecting any element on the PSD. In the blue box that appears, click the arrow on the far right. In the next dialog, give the image a name and choose a file format. If you so choose, there's even a 2x option at the bottom for high-density displays.

At this point, you might assume that choosing Save downloads the image. However, the image makes a pit stop in your Assets tab over in the right sidebar, from which you can then download the image. Why the middle man? Extract adds it to your Creative Cloud assets for easy sharing with your team or retrieving later (see **Figure 9.15**). This is genius. Often, client logos or vital UI pieces end up becoming permanent residents of my Downloads folder. If I'm extracting assets for a project, odds are someone else on my team can use them as well, or I'll just end up losing them in a sea of other files. By proactively and automatically organizing my assets as I extract them, Adobe is providing both a safeguard and a reference.

Figure 9.15 Hey, where'd my download go? Check for it in your Assets tab on the right.

Fortunately, extracted images aren't dumped in one huge folder of assets; rather, they're placed in a folder specific to current PSD's name.

Extracting Values

By default, anything you download from Extract is an image, but images don't represent all that we're trying to extract on their own. We're also interested in fonts and colors.

You'll find a list of fonts used in your PSD in the right sidebar, under Fonts. If the font happens to be sourced by Typekit, clicking the Typekit icon will bring you to the representative font page on Typekit's site. In addition to font name, the Font inspector displays the various sizes used within the entire document, which may be handy when attempting to create a style guide.

Likewise, colors are listed in the right sidebar (see **Figure 9.16**). Extract scans your document and displays swatches of solids and gradients to choose from. Clicking one will show you where in the PSD the colors originated from. Additionally, color options are given within a pop-up dialog, such as Color Mode (RGB, Hex, and HSL) for easy copying. Again, this is super-helpful for establishing a style guide.

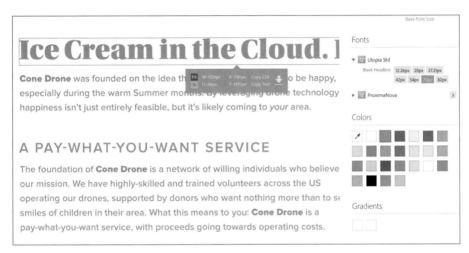

Figure 9.16 Fonts and colors (and gradients) can be plucked from the Styles tab.

Generating CSS

Extract provides suggested CSS in multiple places, in an effort to make the transition from Photoshop to code even easier. The first and most prominent place is at the top of the Styles tab. Choose an element from the PSD to see its CSS generated here.

At the least, each element will have a height and width specified, which you may opt not to use with the goal of flexible media. Remember, neither Extract nor Photoshop can assume responsive web design, so any height, width, or relational space between objects are given relative to a fixed-width canvas. Type will have font family, weight, and size specified, while vector and raster graphics can have background colors and much more.

The second place you can grab CSS from is within the blue box that originates from choosing an element. Toward the right is a Copy All option, which, predictably, copies the CSS straight to your clipboard (see **Figure 9.17**).

Figure 9.17 Additionally, click the Copy All button to send the CSS straight to your clipboard.

Photoshop's CSS Generation

In addition to Extract, Photoshop also has a Copy CSS function you may not have noticed. It's located under Layer in your menu bar (see **Figure 9.18**).

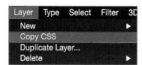

Figure 9.18 It's been around for a little while now, but many people are unfamiliar with pulling CSS straight from Photoshop.

To be fair, I don't recommend relying on the CSS generated by either application blindly. A best practice of writing CSS is to be as concise and succinct as possible, and unfortunately, Photoshop and Extract won't take into account other elements on the canvas when it returns CSS for one. For example, you may have two boxes with exactly the same dimensions, drop shadows, borders, and rounded corners, except one has a red background and the other blue. **Figure 9.19** shows how Photoshop will write the CSS for each.

Here is perhaps a more efficient way: leveraging a class to one difference between the two boxes instead of duplicating all of the same attributes (see **Figure 9.20**).

Photoshop and Extract will get you quite far with the CSS they generate, but you'll want to go back and check how you may be able to make it more efficient in the context of other elements.

```
13   .box {
14       border-radius: 10px;
15       background-color: rgb(220, 228, 245);
16       box-shadow: 3px 5px 0px rgba(197, 208, 232, 0.4);
17       position: absolute;
18       left: 412px;
19       top: 1716px;
20       width: 216px;
21       height: 61px;
22       z-index: 92;
23   }
24
25
26   .box-2 {
27       border-radius: 10px;
28       background-color: rgb(220, 228, 245);
29       box-shadow: 3px 5px 0px rgba(197, 208, 232, 0.4);
30       position: absolute;
31       left: 412px;
32       top: 1716px;
33       width: 216px;
34       height: 61px;
35       z-index: 92;
36   }
```

Figure 9.19 Completely accurate CSS, just a bit redundant

```
40   .box{
41       border-radius: 10px;
42       background-color: blue;
43       box-shadow: 3px 5px 0px rgba(197, 208, 232, 0.4);
44       width: 216px;
45       height: 61px;
46   }
47
48   .box.red{
49       background-color: red;
50   }
```

Figure 9.20 A more extendable way of displaying boxes and a variable

At this point, you've gotten everything out of Photoshop that you need to and ideally much quicker than you had in the past. Generator and Extract Assets are becoming essential to most Photoshop workflows, no matter the style exercise or comp. I encourage you to get familiar with them since I think you'll be saying goodbye to Save for Web in the near future.

I'm not sure about you, but all this talk about more efficient alternatives has me confident that Photoshop can stay in our workflows—so much so, in fact, that I want to push it further. What else is out there that can speed up the typical Photoshop tasks?

10

EXTENDING PHOTOSHOP

As we've been weaving between Photoshop and the browser, it may have occurred to you that efficiency is of critical importance. It's kind of like when I need to go to Home Depot or when my wife goes to Target: We always know what we need to get, but we'll never get anything done if we spend forever and a day shopping for it.

On its own, Photoshop can be an efficient tool for web design. However, the variety of workflows it needs to support makes it difficult to optimize it for every application. Just think of the different projects and clients we work for. While some of us are designing minimal and flat marketing sites, others are making detailed dashboards and complex interfaces reliant on icons.

I don't know what end of the spectrum you fall on. That's why you might find this chapter the most valuable of the bunch.

Building the "You" Version of Photoshop

If you really want to work efficiently in Photoshop, you'll need to tailor it to your specific needs by leveraging some of the thousands of plug-ins and extensions out there. Trying to find a decent plug-in can be like finding a needle in a haystack. People have been making extensions for Photoshop seemingly forever, so trying to sort through what's valuable and what will infect your computer with a virus can be overwhelming.

Don't fear. I've selected a few of my favorites in this chapter (and I hope I've earned your trust by this point).

Let's break down these helpful tools into the following categories:

▶ *Artwork*: Plug-ins for quicker, easier, and more accurate comping

▶ *Color*: Alternatives to the baked-in color picker

▶ *Assets*: Plug-ins that generate icons and code

▶ *Prototyping*: Useful services for infusing interactivity

▶ *Organization*: Utilities for keeping things tidy

If you're like me, you may have the impulse to use this as a checklist and install every last one. I can't speak to what that might do to the performance of Photoshop or your computer, but I can say that it's probably not the most effective way to customize Photoshop. The way to get the most use out of these plug-ins is to find the ones that will help you the most and just keep the rest on your radar for a time when you might need them in the future. Having too many options for workflow efficiency can be confusing and actually slow you down (not that I've had that happen or anything).

I won't guarantee it, but I'm confident at least one of these extensions will significantly change the way you use Photoshop for the better.

Staying Up-to-Date with Extending Photoshop

For the longest time, people would ask me what plug-ins I used, and I had no answer for them—for no other reason than I forgot the names of the ones I did. With Photoshop, as with anything else in this industry, it's ridiculously difficult to stay on top of what's new, what's good, and what's coming. It would be helpful to have a resource that kept track of all of it.

For this reason, I created Extending Photoshop (*www.extendingphotoshop .com*), a collection of tools, methods, and ideas for efficiency. It's updated often and includes the extensions you'll see in this chapter. You can stay apprised of any additions by following *@extendingps* on Twitter.

Artwork

At the core of what we do in Photoshop is creating artwork. While it's likely you won't find a plug-in out there to do your job for you, there's a handful that can provide shortcuts to finding what you need to make a beautiful design.

Subtle Patterns

www.plugin.subtlepatterns.com

Price: $11.99

If you've ever used textures or background patterns in your artwork, you know how difficult it is to find a reliable collection to choose from. A while ago, I stumbled on Atle Mo's Subtle Patterns, a collection of extremely tastefully done patterns ready to be used on the Web in PNG format or downloaded as a PAT file (Photoshop pattern). While the web app is easy to use, downloading each one individually in Photoshop is an arduous task, to say the least.

The Subtle Patterns plug-in (see **Figure 10.1**) makes the online library available from within Photoshop. Applying patterns is also nondestructive to your original artwork because Subtle Patterns will create a separate Pattern Fill layer for you to manipulate. Other functions of the plug-in include a quick search and a favorites menu.

Figure 10.1 Subtle Patterns puts the best selection of patterns at your fingertips.

CC Market

Before you start scouring the Web for free brushes, vectors, and icons, save yourself some sanity by checking out the Creative Cloud Market (see **Figure 10.2**). It's accessible from within your Creative Cloud panel in the menu bar.

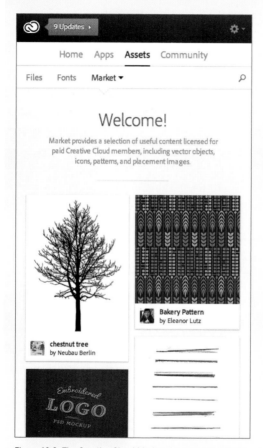

Figure 10.2 The Creative Cloud Market should be your first stop when searching for small assets.

The market comprises contributions from artists around the globe, and I've found it to be of much higher quality than any free asset site. It's included in your Creative Cloud subscription and fully licensed for your personal and commercial work. It's a little-known resource that could end up being a crucial part of your next project.

Random User Generator

www.randomuser.me/photoshop.html

Price: Free

What bothers me most when I see an unsolicited redesign of an application like Facebook is the use of cheesy, albeit perfect, stock photography for user content. We've all done it to some extent before: searched Google Images for a profile picture or snagged one from iStockPhoto.com. It's true that these are often just placeholder images, but while we may be showing what's ideal, is it realistic? Does the design hold up with "ordinary" photos?

The creators of Random User (*www.randomuser.me*) created a free service to provide designers with realistic user data and integrated it with Photoshop with their plug-in, Random User Generator (see **Figure 10.3**). If you design apps or dashboard interfaces, this is an essential extension to have in your toolkit.

Figure 10.3 Random User Generator gives you realistic avatars for your realistic app.

Social Kit

http://socialkit.madebysource.com

Price: Free

Granted, Social Kit (see **Figure 10.4**) has a very specific use case, but it's worth including. If you're in charge of maintaining your company's social media presence or need to show a client what theirs might look like, this plug-in will save you boatloads of time.

Figure 10.4 With Social Kit you get social network profile templates without the pain of creating them from scratch.

Because there are no sandboxes to preview design tweaks to a social network profile, comping in Photoshop is your best option. Instead of creating a blank profile from scratch or struggling to find what free Facebook template is up-to-date, Social Kit does the work for you. Just select the network and template you need from the plug-in panel and cry happy tears as you save 20 minutes of work re-creating a template that's bound to be obsolete in the next month or two.

Pictura

http://pictura.madebysource.com

Price: Free

I'm sure you're all familiar with the process of finding a placeholder photo from a stock site, saving it to your desktop, and opening it in Photoshop. It's not an incredibly inefficient process, but being able to stay in one environment instead of three would be helpful.

Pictura (see **Figure 10.5**) is a free plug-in from Source that brings the photography stored on Flickr into Photoshop. The convenience of searching from within Photoshop is magnified only when you consider how strong Flickr is as a stock photo resource. Because Pictura allows you to filter by license, you have a legitimate photo asset library without ever needing to jump out to the browser.

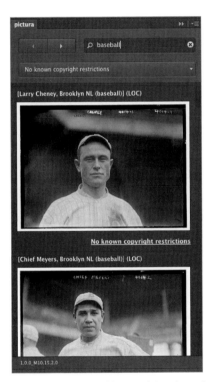

Figure 10.5 Pictura provides complete and seamless Flickr integration.

Transform Each

http://blog.kam88.com/en/transform-each-beta-script.html

Price: Free

Each Adobe application has its little quirks, and the transform functions in Illustrator and Photoshop are great examples. Whereas Illustrator allows you to resize multiple items and maintain their horizontal and vertical origins, Photoshop takes the group of items and resizes from the collective center.

Kamil Khadeyev, who runs a fantastic blog aptly named Captain Awesome, made a script for Photoshop called Transform Each (see **Figure 10.6**) that will emulate the Illustrator transformation of each item. It's a small quirk to be sure but one that could save you a lot of time nevertheless.

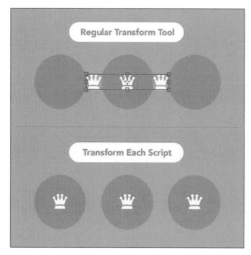

Figure 10.6 Transform Each brings the transform flexibility of Illustrator to Photoshop.

DevRocket

www.devrocket.uiparade.com

Price: $19 for a personal license, $99 for teams

DevRocket (see **Figure 10.7**) is the quintessential time-saving extension if you design apps for iOS. It's as multifaceted as it is beautifully crafted. Its primary functions include premade canvas settings and templates for all iOS device sizes, presets for each icon size, native previews, and easy asset generation for 1x, 2x, and 3x resolutions.

My favorite of the bunch are the native preview options since it's so easy to design in a silo environment with no context for how a screen would look on an iPhone, how an icon would look like on a home screen, or how information would look on the App Store. With a few clicks, you can preview your work in any of these beautifully rendered contexts.

Figure 10.7 Speeding up your iOS workflow is easy with DevRocket.

Bjango Actions

www.bjango.com/articles/actions

Price: Free

Bjango cofounder Marc Edwards is as much of an authority on Photoshop as you'll find anywhere, and he knows a thing or two about proper file setup. He's created a series of Photoshop actions (see **Figure 10.8**) to save you tons of time on small tasks such as creating backgrounds, resizing assets, and modifying the size of your canvas.

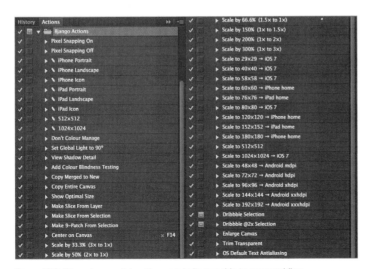

Figure 10.8 Bjango's one-click actions are indispensable to your workflow.

These actions are so comprehensive that it would be silly to list them here, so do yourself a favor and download them today.

WebZap

http://webzap.uiparade.com

Price: $19 for a personal license, $99 for teams

Should you find yourself in need of comping a layout (hey, I never said you couldn't, just that there are better ways of bringing your clients into the design process), you can save yourself a lot of time by using WebZap from Norm Sheeran of UI Parade (see **Figure 10.9**). WebZap comes complete with some useful premade layouts to get designing instead of deer-stuck-in-the-headlights phase when you open a blank document.

Figure 10.9 WebZap provides web layouts on your screen in a "zap," I suppose.

Nestled in WebZap is an incredibly useful feature for text styling that allows you to assign HTML tags like `<h1>`, `<h2>`, and `<p>` for easy global formatting. It's similar to character styles, but I especially appreciate the nod to web nomenclature.

Composer

www.jasonforal.com/composer

Price: Free

If you use Layer Comps (I'm more of a Smart Objects kind of guy), you've probably noticed that it's hard to keep control over shared elements between them. Any layers you change on one aren't reflected on others, but sometimes that's not advantageous for editing multiple Layer Comps at once.

Jason Foral developed Composer as a script to solve this challenge (see **Figure 10.10**). Composer is a set of four commands that give you the control that's missing natively over Layer Comps: the ability to update layer effects, position, visibility, or all three.

Figure 10.10 Composer is a great plug-in for extending layer comps.

Layout Wrapper

http://blog.kam88.com/en/layout-wraper-for-photoshop.html

Price: Free

Too easily lost in our Photoshop artwork is the presentation of it. Just as DevRocket gives you a preview of iOS environments, Layout Wrapper frames your work in a Safari browser (see **Figure 10.11**). It's a small detail to be certain, but presenting your Photoshop work in the context it will live in is a best practice of web design. This script makes it painless.

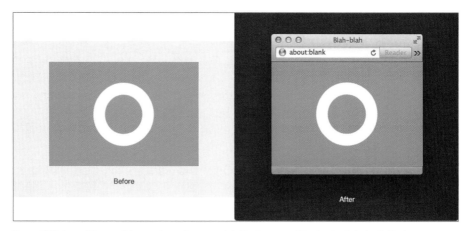

Figure 10.11 LayoutWrapper lets you show off your work in the browser, without actually being in the browser.

RotateMe

http://blog.kam88.com/en/rotateme-photoshop-actions.html

Price: Free

When you try to rotate a path in Photoshop, you wind up with jagged edges. If you haven't noticed this phenomenon, draw a rectangle, give it a thick stroke like a photo frame would have, and then rotate it. That stair-stepping along the edges is less than ideal, and workarounds tend to involve rasterizing your vectors prior to rotation. No, thank you.

RotateMe (see **Figure 10.12**) is a Photoshop action that smooths these unsightly edges while still maintaining vector status. It's particularly handy for icon designers who use rotation in Photoshop to achieve various shapes.

Figure 10.12 Jagged edges are a thing of the past with RotateMe.

Color

Choosing the right color in Photoshop isn't always the easiest task. The default color picker is adequate, but extending it to make a cohesive palette is downright impossible, so we'll need to look elsewhere. Although some of these options are solely browser-based, they do allow quick copy functions to get you right back into Photoshop.

0to255

www.0to255.com

Price: Free

0to255 is my color picker of choice (see **Figure 10.13**). If you have a similar style and choose primarily monochromatic color schemes for your interfaces, having the hex values for lighter and darker shades of a base color is essential. Lighter shades can map to hover states of links and buttons, while darker shades can be used as backgrounds.

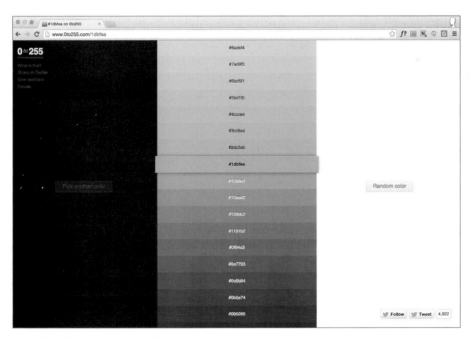

Figure 10.13 Finally, a sensible variation picker!

TIP Defining these values is easily achieved in Sass via mixins. For example, using color: darken($purple, 20); will darken the defined color purple by 20 percent.

0to255 is a color variation app by Shaun Chapman that displays shades of a color, lightening to white and darkening to black in increments of 3 percent. Macaw is the only design app I've seen to integrate this type of selection in its native color picker, and while it may be destined for Photoshop one day, 0to255.com is a great tab to keep open in your browser.

Adobe Color (formerly Kuler)

http://color.adobe.com

Price: Free for everyone, but only Adobe ID holders can save palettes

Crowdsourcing color palettes can be a beautiful thing, especially when so many people end up contributing. With seemingly endless options, Adobe Color is a vast collection of online themes that can be synced to apps like Photoshop and Illustrator (see **Figure 10.14**). Similarly, any themes created within Photoshop can be saved and made available to the public through the web app. If nothing else, playing with the color wheel is a hoot.

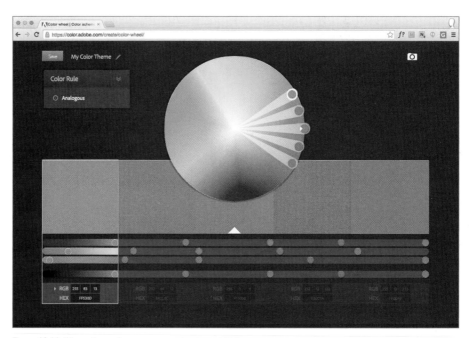

Figure 10.14 Why not crowdsource your next color palette?

Adobe Color CC for iOS

http://adobe.com/products/color.html

Price: Free

If you've ever stood in awe of a beautiful sunset, magnificent artwork, or the view atop a mountain (who hasn't?), your designer brain can't help but long to derive a color palette. An iOS device and Adobe Color CC (see **Figure 10.15**) make it all possible—just snap a photo with your camera and pull out those inspiring tones.

Figure 10.15 Inspired by the world around you? Capture its color like you would Pokemon.

Adobe Color CC is a companion app to the web version with the same name, which means you'll be able to share the themes you capture from your iPhone. If it sounds somewhat useful to you, give it a try. It's way more addicting than you could possibly imagine.

Coolorus

www.coolorus.com

Price: $11.99 for a single license (two computers)

If terms like *gamut*, *harmony*, and *luminosity* get you excited, you'll most certainly want snag Coolorus (see **Figure 10.16**). If the native color options in Photoshop lack the control you seek, this is your plug-in, without a doubt.

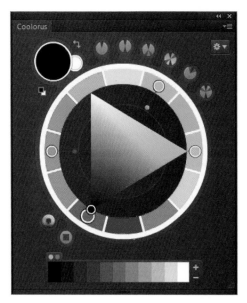

Figure 10.16 If you're looking to geek out on color, Coolorus is your plug-in.

Coolorus has tons of modes and features for creating robust palettes or adjusting color on the canvas. Do you recall my crush on 0to255's shade picker? That's just one of Coolorus' options. Sadly, Coolorus has had a difficult time transitioning to the HTML5-based panels of CC 2014, but a promise of its development is enough to color me, and many others, intrigued.

Assets

Asset integration, inspiration, and generation are common features of Photoshop extensions, but there are some truly helpful ones in the bunch. With the growing popularity of icon services, you can bet there's some decent Photoshop integration.

Additionally, the fact that Photoshop can generate CSS is surely a sign of the times. Some plug-in developers have taken this a step further, as you can imagine, and created similar generation functions for different needs.

iOS Hat

www.ioshat.madebysource.com

Price: $19.99

It's wild that tools exist to translate the Photoshop canvas to complex programming languages. Foremost among these tools is iOS Hat (see **Figure 10.17**), which should appeal to any of the following audiences: iOS developers who inherit PSDs, designers looking to learn the basics of Objective-C and/or Swift, and unicorns who develop their own iOS app designs.

Figure 10.17 iOS Hat generates iOS code from your PSD. Mind blown, indeed.

iOS Hat has two primary functions. The first, titled Generate, allows you to extract code or PNGs ready for implementation. The second, titled Measure, provides code for dimensions and spatial relationships. iOS Hat is truly impressive and worth looking into, even if you're just curious about how your design gets coded by someone else.

OtherIcons

http://othericons.madebysource.com

Price: Plug-in is free; individual icon sets vary from free to $10 each

Jumping out to the browser to find icons can be a hassle, especially when you're in a nice groove designing in Photoshop. Icon community OtherIcons has a plug-in that brings its content conveniently into a Photoshop panel for you to peruse (see **Figure 10.18**).

Figure 10.18 OtherIcons is a lovely collection of icons from numerous sources.

Icon packs vary in price, though there are some that are free to get you started. The quality of the icons makes it quite possible that Othericons eliminates your Photoshop-to-browser-to-Photoshop icon workflow.

Glifo

http://glifo.uiparade.com

Price: $19 for a personal license, $99 for teams

Icon fonts have become a popular alternative to placing tons of individual <img> tags. If you're detailing your icons in Photoshop, Glifo makes packaging them up easy as pie. Select all your icon layers and then click Create Icon Font in Glifo's panel, and your Glifo will generate a serviceable icon font (see **Figure 10.19**).

Figure 10.19 Pack all your icons up in a nifty web font by using Glifo.

It's as simple as it sounds. Have fun with all the time you saved not having to export each individual asset.

FlatIcon

www.flaticon.com

Price: Free with account

For personal projects or ones with modest budgets, free icons are undoubtedly appealing. FlatIcon is a community of icons sourced by more than 50 authors, and their plug-in brings 500+ icon packs to Photoshop for your convenience (see **Figure 10.20**). Don't underestimate the quality of the content, either.

Figure 10.20 You've never seen so many free icons in one place as you will in FlatIcon. Now it's in Photoshop.

TinyPNG

www.tinypng.com/photoshop

Price: Free

TinyPNG (see **Figure 10.21**) is a web app that will take your PNGs from Photoshop and magically reduce their size through some black-magic compression methods. Having relied on this service for years, you could imagine my excitement when I found out the company offers this app as a Photoshop plug-in.

Figure 10.21 TinyPNG compresses PNGs to squeeze out every last byte of potential savings.

Unlike other extensions that appear in panels, TinyPNG is an Export option found by going to File > Export > TinyPNG. Since it's not currently integrated with Generator, it'll take some scripting to automate its use, but it's totally possible.

ImageOptim

www.imageoptim.com

Price: Free

ImageOptim (see **Figure 10.22**) is a Mac app for compressing any image file and in some cases drastically reducing file size. It's a good practice to run your exported assets through ImageOptim before using them on a live site.

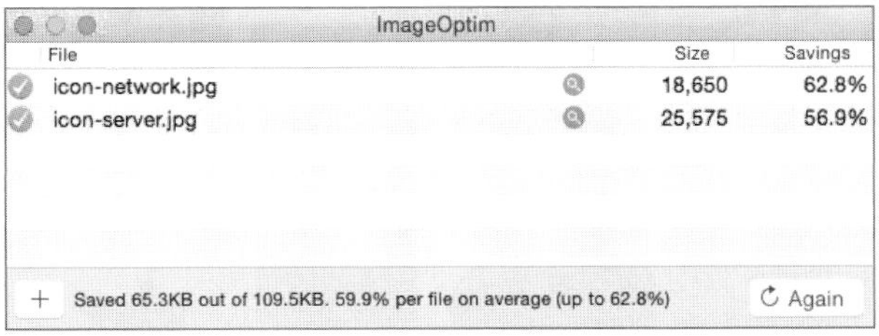

ImageOptim			
File		Size	Savings
✓ icon-network.jpg	🔍	18,650	62.8%
✓ icon-server.jpg	🔍	25,575	56.9%
+ Saved 65.3KB out of 109.5KB. 59.9% per file on average (up to 62.8%)			↻ Again

Figure 10.22 Use ImageOptim to knock the fat out of semi-compressed image files.

Even if the time savings are low, your pages will load a fraction quicker, which could make all the difference between someone sticking around or leaving.

Prototyping

When we looked at Photoshop's pain points in Chapter 2, lack of interactivity was a major one. While there's still a facade between Photoshop and the browser, some services provide unique ways of previewing your content. Also, here's a fun fact: Each one of these prototyping services leverages Adobe Generator.

Framer, Composite, and Stand In

www.framerjs.com

Price: $79.99

www.getcomposite.com

Price: $9.99 in the iTunes App Store

www.standin.io

Price: $25/month for individuals, $100/month for teams of five and more

Framer (see **Figure 10.23**), Composite (see **Figure 10.24**), and Stand In (see **Figure 10.25**) take Photoshop artwork and create mobile prototypes that are ready for interaction on a connected device. iOS and Android designers will find these tools especially useful for previewing screenflows without needing to commit to development. The differences between the apps are subtle, and in the case of Framer, Photoshop integration is just one of many features. Fortunately, each product has a free demo or trial.

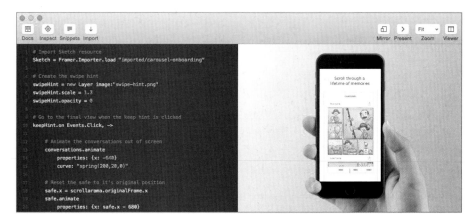

Figure 10.23 Framer is a robust tool for creating interactive and animated prototypes.

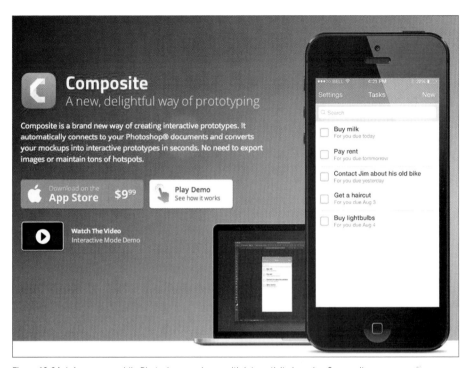

Figure 10.24 Infuse your mobile Photoshop mock-ups with interactivity by using Composite.

Figure 10.25 Preview mobile screens on mobile devices with Stand In. It just makes sense.

InVision

www.invisionapp.com

Price: Free for your first project; plans range from $15/month (3 projects) to $100/month (unlimited projects and team use)

InVision has truly taken the design industry by storm recently, and considering their pedigree of customers, it's no wonder. Companies like Adobe, Airbnb, Yahoo, eBay, and Evernote all use InVision to prototype Photoshop artwork prior to development. Whereas the previous prototyping tools I mentioned are mobile-specific, InVision will add interactivity to any size design.

Beyond their prototyping service, InVision offers a free Photoshop plug-in named LiveShare (see **Figure 10.26**), and it's quite magical. Whereas traditional screenshare tools lack the means for on-screen annotation and collaboration, LiveShare is chock-full of such features. Not only can invitees draw and type on your mirrored comp, but you can hop back into Photoshop, make a change on the fly, and see it reflected in the meeting.

Figure 10.26 InVision LiveShare is the plug-in your distributed team has been missing.

Just think of how incredibly helpful this is for teams with remote employees who can't gather around someone's desk in the office to critique or offer art direction.

Organization

I'm not sure working in Photoshop has ever been a tidy operation by default. Much effort goes into constructing a design in an easy manner you can reference later. Here are some fun ways of automating some rather mundane processes.

GuideGuide

www.guideguide.me

Price: Free

A little while back, a hilarious GIF went around where a designer was trying to place a guide and, because of snapping, they kept placing it a pixel either above or below their desired value. It's a frustration most of us share because the smallest flick of the wrist immediately after releasing the mouse can derail an otherwise perfectly placed guide.

Cameron McEfee is a life-saver. His plug-in, aptly named GuideGuide, will place guides based on numeric values, selections, or mathematic equations (see **Figure 10.27**). Simply put, it takes the guesswork out of a task where precision is essential.

Figure 10.27 No more wrestling with guides!

Renamy

www.renamy.com

Price: Free

Renamy (see **Figure 10.28**) is a mass-layer renaming plug-in sure to help keep you organized. More importantly, Renamy is a practical way to set up your PSD for Generator's extraction of assets.

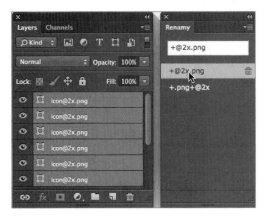

Figure 10.28 Renamy is a great tool for batch-renaming multiple layers.

Ink

www.ink.chrometaphore.com

Price: Free

If you're handing off an element collage or comp to another designer or developer, chances are they're looking to grab style information. While Extract is a great way to accomplish the task, Ink from Chrometaphore will detail design specifications on a separate layer (technically, a folder) of your PSD (see **Figure 10.29**).

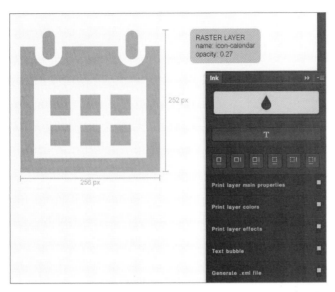

Figure 10.29 Use Chrometaphore's Ink to bake style documentation into your PSD.

Ink is the ultimate documentation plug-in for Photoshop since it grabs specs on type, effects, color, and dimensions. For a developer who doesn't have Photoshop, providing them an exported static image with Ink's documentation is genius.

psdiff

http://filp.github.io/psdiff

Price: Free

If your team uses GitHub, you probably have PSDs hanging around your project repositories with no way to preview them like you would HTML & CSS files. Better yet, GitHub doesn't provide an easy way to track their changes.

psdiff is a brilliant fix to this problem (see **Figure 10.30**). It's a tool you can install as a Git hook, which will export a PNG any time a PSD is saved. Now, anyone on your team can see the latest state of a PSD without ever having to open Photoshop.

Figure 10.30 Finally, PSD previews in GitHub!

Miscellaneous Photoshoppery

While every tool covered so far can bring efficiency to your workflow, none of them can make you more proficient in Photoshop on its own. Becoming a Photoshop ninja takes time, and there are some really fun sites dedicated to helping you learn it backward and forward.

ShortcutFoo

www.shortcutfoo.com/app/dojos/photoshop-mac

Price: Free

ShortcutFoo (see **Figure 10.31**) is one of my favorite web apps for no other reason than I'm hilariously bad at keyboard shortcuts. Trust me, if you think you're good, Shortcut Foo will most likely put you to shame.

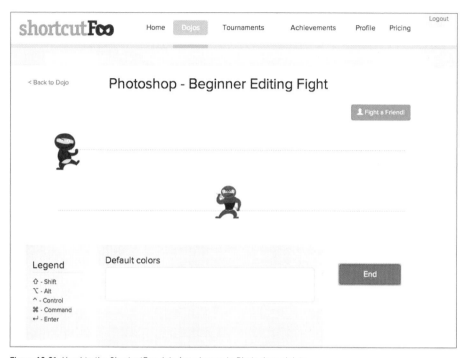

Figure 10.31 Head to the ShortcutFoo dojo for a lesson in Photoshop ninjutsu.

It's an entertaining way to learn some impressive keyboard moves spread over three stages: Learn, Fight, and Test. The Learn phase is no-pressure, at-your-own-pace instruction. Fight puts you up against the computer in a duel that Bruce Lee would have difficulty with. Test is the final exam to prove your mastery. Shortcut Foo also has courses for the command line and Git, among others, in case you really want to impress your friends.

Photoshop Secrets

http://photoshopsecrets.tumblr.com

Price: Free

Edward Sanchez does a fantastic job keeping his readership up-to-date with little-known features and tricks on his blog, Photoshop Secrets (see **Figure 10.32**). His posts include detailed tutorials and simple links to useful tools to circumvent lengthy workflows.

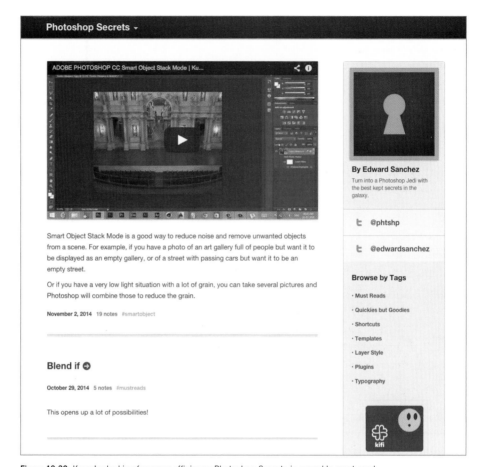

Figure 10.32 If you're looking for some efficiency, Photoshop Secrets is a weekly must-read.

Phew. The amazing thing is, this list only scratches the surface of the array of amazing Photoshop extensions currently available, so if there's a specific pain point of your workflow, you can most likely find a plug-in to help. With most offered for free or at modest price points, these small add-ons can save you significant time.

Of course, there are some process points you can adjust to save more time that have nothing to do with Photoshop's features or extensions, as you'll discover in Chapter 11.

11

REMEMBERING ETIQUETTE

I almost quit.

A while back, I worked at an agency where the process was generally as follows: The marketing people would meet with a client at the start of a project and then relay some information to the creative director, who would have first dibs on designing the site. He'd make a few PSD comps and hand them down to me to quality-check, more or less, to see whether everything he was doing was achievable in code. As the web designer, I was the bridge between "creative" and development.

I probably don't need to point out that my role in the process should have started long before inheriting a PSD, but even that didn't bother me much at the time. The role came with enough freedom to change what I saw fit that I couldn't complain too much. Prior to learning how to design in the browser, I was lightning-quick at making edits in Photoshop (I'd like to think I still am). It was a skill I took much pride in.

That's why it surprised everyone that my involvement derailed every project timeline.

The Problem with Inheriting PSDs

I would spend hours, and I mean hours, just getting myself up to speed when I received a batch of PSDs. *Which file should I be using? Why is your Franklin Gothic different from mine, and is that OK? I can't find any of the purchased stock photos. Why does that drop shadow look like there's a spotlight aimed at my monitor?*

Why did we bolt down the tables so I can't flip them anymore?

That's why I almost quit. The time I would spend making sense of a PSD was equal to the amount of time I'd spend on actual design. I venture to guess you've been in a similar situation, inheriting PSDs from someone and forming 25 questions before you even touch a pixel. If you haven't, count your lucky stars.

The friction between designer and developer—or, in this case, designer and designer—is enough to produce unhealthy angst and discord. You could follow all of the workflow advice in this book to the letter, but if you work on a team that allows the distribution of messy PSDs, you won't be getting any more efficient any time soon. If you care about such things (and you must, to have read ten chapters about it so far), a toxic and inefficient process will have you looking elsewhere for employment.

Having thought I was the only one in this kind of situation, I made a text document that outlined all of the things I'd like to have tidied up prior to inheriting artwork. It wasn't asking much for someone to name their layers, right? Before I clicked Send on a companywide email, I realized this would die the same death just about every other piece of internal documentation does. *No, this needs to be taken more seriously. It needs to look more official. This has to be a website.*

And so I created one. This is the origin story of the Photoshop Etiquette Manifesto for Web Designers (see **Figure 11.1**).

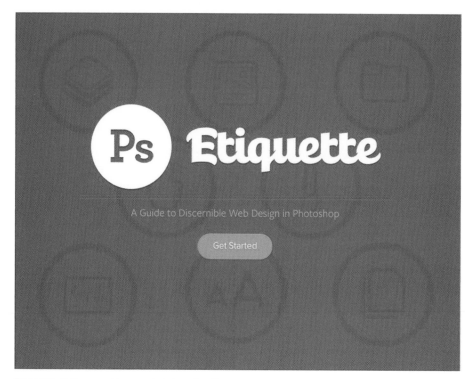

Figure 11.1 So it was, and is: *www.photoshopetiquette.com*

What Is Photoshop Etiquette?

To my surprise, designers from seemingly all over the world lauded having this kind of documentation. That's when I realized these process pain points were ones everyone could relate to. Assuming we all have different workflows, etiquette must be the common ingredient that's missing.

When we discuss etiquette, it's typically framed around dinner table manners. Having etiquette means you're proper, considerate, and dignified. Not having it means you're sloppy, selfish, and, dare I say, immature. Etiquette (or the lack of it) in web design, specifically in Photoshop, has the same characteristics. You either can be mindful of the next person to inherit your file or can work with reckless abandon because you may think it's quicker to do so.

What does having Photoshop etiquette look like? This chapter will dive deep into some examples, including best practices for file organization, layer organization, image and type considerations, using effects, and proofing your work. Don't worry, we can all be better in this area of design, myself included. By the end of the chapter you'll have a great reference for making some helpful adjustments and choices, and if you're the type who's already on top of things, you'll have some required reading to pass around to your team.

Photoshop etiquette is critical to any team and any workflow. Here is a look at some reasons why.

Improves Efficiency

The most important benefit of employing Photoshop etiquette is to make a dent in some of the time lost transferring PSDs. Whether it's a preemptive list of disclaimers by the transferrer or a myriad of questions by the transferee, design team members spend a considerable amount of time just getting familiar with a mock-up. The least you can do is limit these conversations to being client- or project-oriented (*What was the stakeholder's response to the blue background here?*) instead of technical (*Does this background need to have the Pattern Overlay turned on?*).

Keeps You Organized

It should be apparent that if you were to tidy up your files, layers, and assets, someone wouldn't need to spend so much time sifting through everything (see **Figure 11.2**). The greater benefit is that employing better organization helps *you* most of all. For those times when you're called on to create an asset or find the latest version of a PSD, you owe it to yourself to keep everything in order. Being organized in Photoshop is a gift from you to your future self.

Figure 11.2 Using folders in and out of Photoshop makes for easy scanning and findability.

Creates Conventions

An undervalued benefit of adhering to these guidelines is that you're establishing common methods and conventions for the team to align to: *Here's the way we name our files. This is how we use folders in our PSDs. This is where we put stock photography.* When you create standards for such things, your file and PSD structures look similar from project to project.

Increased Importance in an RWD Workflow

Think about the number of files that comprise a website. I'm not sure about you, but I use more PSDs, CSS, and images now than I did pre-RWD. Significantly more.

Now, consider all the hands that touch said files. Creative directors, art directors, interface designers, front-end developers, clients...and the list goes on. The art of building websites involves many moving pieces between breakpoint-specific CSS or Retina versions of images. It's not that RWD is inherently messy; it just demands that we support and consider devices and views we hadn't before. Keeping everything organized requires discipline.

It's not easy to stay on top of everything, but clarity in Photoshop should be nonnegotiable. In other words, we have enough to worry about to then have to chase one another to interpret what's happening in a PSD. RWD has only placed greater emphasis on staying organized and increased efficiency on our teams.

Without further ado, let's break down what it good Photoshop etiquette looks like.

Files

Before you start clarifying your layers and artwork, the least you can do is apply some discipline when you're organizing files and folders. A well-constructed directory sets the tone for the quality of the contents inside it. If your filenames run rampant and empty folders are strewn across the project, it will affect my perception of the artwork when I eventually find it. If I don't have confidence in your file structure, I won't feel confident about the contents of your PSD. Don't overlook file organization; it's the best way to convey that you're on top of everything.

Name Files Appropriately

Client-homepage-Final-v4.psd

Product-interior-v2-2-DO_NOT_USE_THIS_ONE.psd

We designers are pretty funny if you think about it. In an effort to aide communication, we try to convey the intent of our PSDs through the field name (see **Figure 11.3**). Why do we make it so hard on ourselves? Is "Final-v4" really final? Is any file meant for the ever-changing Web "final" anyway? Should we have to note which files are meant to be used and which ones not through suffixes like "DO_NOT_USE" or "OLD"?

Figure 11.3 Do the red labels (top) mean "danger" like I think they do, or is Latest_Latest accurate too? Instead, let's keep it simple (bottom).

Commit to establishing clarity in your filenames. Simplify any files that you and your collaborators need: "Project-View.psd." That's it.

You should also resolve to archive any artwork you don't need instead of keeping it around with a funky file name. If Project-View.psd needs updating but you don't want to lose the first version, create a copy and store it in a folder called "_archive" or similar. This practice will help someone inheriting a file structure find what they need quickly and have confidence that they're opening the right PSD.

Store Assets Relative to PSD

Pretty high up on the list of web design annoyances is the endless search for the icons, stock photos, and illustrations someone's using in a PSD. I totally see them in the artwork, but when I need the originals, where are they? Do I need to ask you to fish through the sea that is your desktop and email them to me? If so, we're probably going to have some discord.

Similar to packaging InDesign files, you should include a folder of every asset that didn't find its origins in the PSD. My recommendation is to store this folder in the same directory as the PSD (see **Figure 11.4**).

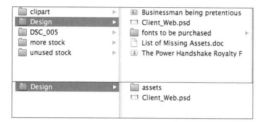

Figure 11.4 Needle-in-a-haystack asset organization (top) is a questionable practice. Tidy it up with a dedicated assets folder.

In doing so, you'll circumvent having to stop what you're doing to find the stock photo in your Downloads folder. Win-win.

File Accessibility

In a similar vein, it's critical for any and all project files to find their way to a shared repository. On one project I needed a PSD on a Friday but someone had forgotten to put it on the shared file server. If this happens every now and then, that's not so bad, but if it's a habit, then it's a problem.

The easiest way to ensure all your artwork is on a file share is to work directly off of one. You will run some risk of losing your work, just as you would be if your computer went down unexpectedly. At least on the file share you (typically) have greater assurance of a backup. Even more reliable is using version control, such as Git and a service like GitHub, to keep all your files up-to-date and accessible.

Working locally and remembering to upload files occasionally is hard but not impossible. It helps to set yourself an alert for the end of the day.

Layers

Layers are the core of Photoshop etiquette. The majority of the offenses I've endured with inherited work resulted from messy, unclear layers. Having to spend time renaming and reorganizing layers is like being a parent who has to clean up their child's room. If you can teach them to clean it themselves, or not to make such a mess in the first place, you'll be able to get done all the other stuff on your list.

If you're looking to take some baby steps with etiquette, do these first. Trust me, they make a world of difference.

Name Layers and Be Accurate

Accurate layer naming is the quintessential rule of Photoshop etiquette. We need to rid the world of "Layer 0 copy copy." That's simply not useful.

Instead, try to be deliberate with every layer name in your document. If it's a photo, don't just name it "photo." Tell your collaborators *which* photo. If it's a button, "Shape 1" isn't clear enough; there may be 25 other shapes nearby. Consider naming the foundation of an efficient collaborative workflow and build upon it by naming accurately.

Similarly, attempt to name assets for their intended use in an interface. If a background belongs to a footer, why not name the layer "footer-bg"? If you recall how Generator works to take layer names and produce files, incorporating a layer's intended use into its name makes this a no-brainer. Name it "footer-bg.jpg" and save yourself the work of renaming extracted assets later (see **Figure 11.5**).

TIP If you want to get rid of the "copy" suffix Photoshop automatically puts on new layers, click the Panel Options icon in the upper right of the Layers panel. From there, deselect the Add 'copy' to Copied Layers and Groups check box.

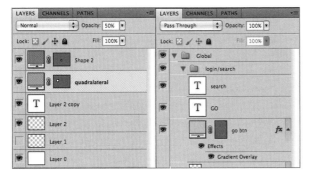

Figure 11.5 We can do better than this (left). Show some pride in your craft by naming your layers (right).

A common argument against naming layers is that it takes too much time. While there's some truth in that, I'd argue the time it takes you, the originator of the PSD, to name your layers is but a fraction of what it takes someone else, who's unfamiliar with your artwork, to identify and name them. Not naming them at all would be downright inefficient when you're trying to find things later, wouldn't it?

Cleanup vs. As-You-Go

Some people prefer to name their layers after they've finished their artwork. While that's a totally viable option, you may choose to name your layers as you create them. Going back and naming every layer seems a bit overwhelming to me, personally, and I might struggle with the motivation to do so at the time. Naming layers as I go seems to keep focus of the greater structure and highlight areas I may need to include potential components or alternatives.

A great way to keep an as-you-go methodology going is to start your project by predetermining the groups you'll need and fill them accordingly. For instance, inside my "footer" group I'll create a rectangle. Already having "footer" labeled gives me the hint to name the shape something ("footer-bg," for instance).

There's no wrong time to name your layers, but you may find it easier to do it as you create them.

Use Groups and Globalize Where Possible

A well-structured layer panel is akin to a welcome mat or table of contents for the person who inherits your work. It says, "Hi there. Before we get started, here are all the categories of things I made. Have a great day."

Groups are the best way to group and organize content, so failing to include them in a PSD makes your lack of organization apparent. Grouping by component gives someone the option to make the grouped layers visible/invisible or move them as a unit when they need to (see **Figure 11.6**). Ungrouped layers tend to be quite difficult to corral, especially when two layers of a component may be distant in the layer panel order.

While you're at it, consider globalizing shared components and masks as best you can. Trying to maintain five copies of a header can be exhausting if it never changes, so keep it in a group above and away from content that shifts appearance. The same can be said for masks: There's no reason to duplicate a common mask across ten layers. Instead, place the mask on the group and allow it to cascade down to its contents.

Figure 11.6 Opening a PSD should read like a table of contents.

Delete Unnecessary Layers

Do you hold on to invisible layers and unused concepts the way you do old sweaters? If so, you might be a layer hoarder.

Unless your intent is to toggle visibility to indicate states or behaviors of a particular component, try to let go of any unused layers. All they end up doing is cluttering the Layers panel and confusing someone as to their role. You may have some very good ideas hiding behind the canvas, so document them elsewhere if you can. But by no means keep unused layers hanging around for someone else to figure out what to do with.

Still unconvinced? Do it for performance's sake: The more layers you have, the slower Photoshop runs. A faster Photoshop should be incentive enough to trim down those layers by cutting the fat of unused ones.

Images

Even in the flat-design era, it's hard to skirt around using photography and illustration in Photoshop. Photo manipulations have long been a key to well-crafted interfaces, so it makes sense that we might revert to some messy habits found in traditional photo editing.

Unfortunately, as a composite gets more and more layered and deep, the less we tend to consider someone else needing to make sense of it. Here are a few things we can do to change that.

Be Nondestructive

No matter how many effects you employ, you should be able to take them all away and find the original unscathed. Who knows if you'll need to adjust the effects down the road? It's best to keep total flexibility in the matter by being "nondestructive" to the original.

For example, if a photo has an unwanted artifact you want to remove, using the Eraser tool would cause irreparable harm to the source. The only option to undo such edits is to hang onto the original asset and include it in the PSD again. Instead, use a mask, which could be hidden or edited later and isn't permanent (see **Figure 11.7**).

Figure 11.7 Make edits and adjustments on a mask or separate layer than the original (left) instead of directly on it (right).

Going Nondestructive with Smart Filters

If you're a fan of using Gaussian Blur, you've probably noticed that it's impossible to adjust the intensity of the blur after you've set it. The same applies for most filters: They compromise the integrity of the original artwork the moment they're applied.

There is an alternative, though it requires converting your layer to a Smart Object by right-clicking the layer and choosing Convert to Smart Object. Then, choose the filter you want to apply from the Filter menu, and you'll see a Smart Filter attribute added to the layer. Double-click it to adjust the filter settings whenever you'd like.

Other nondestructive techniques include not rasterizing vector shapes and using adjustment layers.

Use Blend Modes with Care

While it's true that support for blend modes via CSS is growing, be careful using them with any degree of complexity in Photoshop. It's hard to discern how an effect is achieved from the eye of someone trying to extract assets from your PSD. If you've ever tried saving a layer with a Multiply blend mode with alpha transparency, you know it's not exactly within the realm of possibilities.

Always be thinking about how your complex layering or photo manipulations are exported. If they need to be combined and flattened prior to extraction, let the next person know about it. If you do opt to use blend modes in CSS, it's still important to be able to export an accurate fallback image to achieve the effect in browsers that lack blend mode support.

Be Aware of Resolution and Density

It's the job of the developer *and* the designer to keep up-to-date with the bevy of screen resolutions and pixel densities in the wild. Pleading ignorance as to why your icons look fuzzy on a Retina screen isn't going to fly most times. If you set your PSD up for more comprehensive output of asset sizes, you'll have nothing to worry about.

Extract Assets proved to be a handy tool in Chapter 9, and here you see that the presets for including @2x, @3x, and beyond make for easy production. Whether you choose to upscale or downscale your work, having a complete library of assets and relative sizes has never been more important.

Type

Type is probably the trickiest element to work with in Photoshop. You're displeased with either the rendering, selection, or performance for any number of reasons, though all three of these areas have gotten significantly better with Photoshop CC. Regardless, there's a code of etiquette you should adhere to when using type for the Web.

Standardize Font Access

Missing font dialogs are the worst. They impede your progress before you can even open a PSD. What's worse, it's difficult to resolve them correctly. Sure, Typekit integration helps, but if you're considerate about the fonts you're using, it's easy to grow frustrated from not having the correct one.

Often is the case that co-workers have slightly different versions of fonts (be they from different foundries or release dates), such as Franklin Gothic on my computer and Franklin Gothic ITC on someone else's. Not only may their appearance be different, but the name is different enough to warrant Photoshop throwing a missing font dialog. In an ideal situation, a company buys the requisite amount of licenses for a font and distributes them among the design team, ensuring no conflict. However, with the amount of font scouring most of us like to do, it's highly unrealistic to keep to synced set of fonts across all computers.

Some basic courtesy is required on the part of the PSD creator. If a font can be shared (no license restrictions), include it local to the PSD when you hand it off. If a font needs a license, consider using one that doesn't—or, at the very least, include a note with instructions for finding it.

Don't Stretch Type

Stretching type is more of a design practice crime than an etiquette one. I've yet to see a scenario where horizontally or vertically stretched or squished type made anything look *better* (see **Figure 11.8**). If you need condensed or extended type, you're better off using a font that has one included.

Figure 11.8 Don't do it. Step away from the Free Transform tool.

From a technical standpoint, stretching type in CSS isn't easily achieved. There's most likely a backward, obscure way to do it. But again, would you really want to even if it were easy?

Control Your Text Boxes and Separate Them

One of the biggest frustrations of trying to select layers is when you click a canvas element and Photoshop chooses a different piece of text based on an overblown text box (see **Figure 11.9.**). These too-tall and too-wide text boxes are usually accidental, a product of anticipating more text than necessary. When the empty space overlaps other artwork, PSD inheritors have good reason to take issue with your lack of tidiness.

Figure 11.9 Not much can be gleaned from this joint text box (left). On the other hand, separating like elements makes the task easier (right).

The easiest remedy is to resize text boxes immediately after you're done entering and styling text. Much like renaming layers, you could opt to do so just prior to handoff, but it's a discipline probably best practiced in the moment.

Equally important, keeping your text in separate boxes will help someone looking to extract quick style information. When you combine a headline, subheadline, and body text inside the same block, the font, size, leading (line-height), color, and other characteristics show blank in the Character panel (unless they share any of these values). It takes an extra step of selecting individual text inside the box to determine these values, and while achievable, it's certainly not convenient. You can save someone time and clicks by keeping similar type in its own text box.

TIP Forget to draw a text box before you entered text? No worries: select the layer and choose Type > Convert to Paragraph Text. Need the opposite? Remove a text box by choosing Type > Convert to Point Text.

Effects

Even the best designers can overdo it when it comes to applying effects. Effect etiquette isn't about limiting the amount you use so much as it is about establishing clarity with what the effect does. While it's fun to guess how you made a drop shadow by using Bevel and Emboss, it's not easy for someone to know how to show and hide the effect when exporting.

Use Overlays Appropriately

TIP You can achieve a similar effect by right-clicking a thumbnail and choosing Clip Thumbnails to Layer Bounds.

Shape thumbnails in the Layers panel used to be of bigger visual importance prior to Photoshop CC, where the original color of a shape filled the entire thumbnail.

A white square on the canvas shows up as a white thumbnail in the Layers panel, making it easy to find. The worst thing you can do is use a Color Overlay effect to change it to a red square. The thumbnail color won't update, and someone will be hopelessly glossing through your layers looking for something red, never to find it (**Figure 11.10**).

Figure 11.10 Try not to fool someone by showing them one color in the thumbnail but switching it on the canvas.

If possible, change the color fill of a shape instead of applying a filter. Changing the fill will update the thumbnail, and everyone will be happy. The idea here is to try to be as accurate as possible with thumbnail previews, whether you employ Color, Gradient, or Pattern Overlays. Those hints of color make scanning hundreds of layers that much easier.

Nail Tileable Images

Who doesn't like a repeating background every now and then? We can pull it off with a Pattern Overlay or simply tiling images manually. Whatever method you use, be sure to make it seamless.

When a pattern is even one pixel off, the effect of a seamless background is destroyed. If the task of a developer or designer is to go in and extract such backgrounds, making them fix seams is less than considerate, don't you think? Nail the execution of tileable images so someone else won't have to.

Be Deliberate

The natural impulse when you're using layer effects is to treat them like a checklist. *I'll take a Drop Shadow, Stroke, and Gradient Overlay. Check. Check. Check.* By not adjusting the values, you're depending on the Photoshop defaults, which may not be appropriate or consistent with the design of your project (see **Figure 11.11**).

Historically, the defaults for layer effects have been incredibly gaudy, which was actually a good thing. They emphasized the effect to make its appearance unmistakable, so you knew you were using an effect. Additionally, the appearance was so exaggerated that you had no choice but to edit it to a more tasteful value.

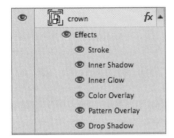

Figure 11.11 Though the Layer Effects panel has the appearance of a wish list, don't treat it like one.

Photoshop CC dialed back such exaggerations in favor of making the defaults fairly tasteful and subtle. While you might be tempted to use their presets, refine the settings to the precise demands of your design instead. A PSD inheritor will appreciate your eye for purpose and consistency, knowing that a 15px blur on a drop shadow was your choice instead of Photoshop's.

QA

When you inherit a PSD from another designer, don't you assume they've performed some basic quality assurance? I know I do, though that's not usually the reality. Being "too close to a design" often means your artwork is wrought with spelling errors and potential content inaccuracies.

It's always wise to give a your PSD one last check before sending it on its way.

Proofread

The majority of the spelling errors I've committed in Photoshop are on huge headlines or buttons high in contrast. Isn't that odd, that the seemingly most apparent elements are often mislooked? It's prudent to start your quality check by looking at the big, noticeable type and working your way down (see **Figure 11.12**).

This is the haedline.

Figure 11.12 Whoops. Missed that one, huh?

Errors within the body copy are less noticeable, and while it's usually understood that Photoshop text isn't final, typos don't communicate the much care for your craft.

Account for All Assets

If stock icons, photography, or illustrations are used in your comps, be sure to purchase them prior to passing around your PSD. Too often someone extracts an asset without any knowledge of its license or potential watermark (see **Figure 11.13**). Those for-placement-only items tend to have a longer shelf life than they should.

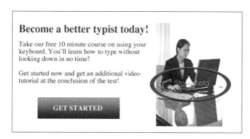

Become a better typist today!

Take our free 10 minute course on using your keyboard. You'll learn how to type without looking down in no time!

Get started now and get an additional video tutorial at the conclusion of the test!

GET STARTED

Figure 11.13 A major faux-pas: leaving the watermark in a photo used on a live site

There are some pretty hilarious, but serious, examples out there of finished artwork with an "iStockPhoto" watermark that made it to production. Make sure this doesn't happen to you by staying on top of purchased assets and updating your PSD.

Be Familiar with Browser Compatibility

While your PSDs usually picture a best-case scenario, the world of Internet Explorer is ignored, and while your extracted assets often accommodate the latest builds of Chrome, Firefox, and Safari, older versions can't use them.

TIP Visit *www.caniuse* *.com* when you're unclear whether a feature or technique is supported in any particular browser.

It's up to you to be familiar with browser support for the effects you display and the assets you export. Not all browsers support SVG, so you'll need to include a fallback PNG. Not all browsers support CSS such as rounded corners and alpha transparency, so you'll need to have a plan for those as well.

Instituting etiquette on your team should prove to be beneficial. Getting everyone on board isn't always easy, but if you want to be master of your craft, the details of a PSD are a good place to start improving. Consistency, clarity, and intent are the elements you need to pour into Photoshop in order for your work to speak for itself.

12

ADOPTING A COMPLETELY NEW WORKFLOW

If you've stuck around this long, congratulations! You have all the pieces of a significantly different workflow. That's probably both very exciting and incredibly scary. I remember the first time we tried element collages at WSOL and were so proud that we'd adopted a new technique. It wasn't long after we started making the first one that I also began to worry about spending too much time on them and thinking, "What happens if the client doesn't get it?"

There are no easy answers to some of the transitional questions that come from hammering out a completely new workflow. This chapter is dedicated to taking a look at how all of the techniques in this book come together and, more importantly, how to institute these changes internally and externally.

Looking Back at Moving Forward

We've covered a lot, and it's easy to lose sight of where everything fits into a process. As we take a quick look back, keep in mind that the takeaways aren't necessarily technical but conceptual. While there's no Make This Responsive button in Photoshop, you can employ intelligent methods of design that make the RWD process more efficient.

Full-Page Photoshop Comps Are Disharmonious with RWD

It's certainly not an absolute rule, but full-page, static comps do very little to help our clients and stakeholders understand the complexities of responsive web design. We're able to show only one moment in time through full-page comps, and any attempt at showing every potential moment, or at least multiple ones, is futile. The static nature of comps also hinders our ability to show design behaviors such as animation, transitions, transforms, hover effects, and more.

Designing in the Browser Helps, But Not As Much As We'd Like

The browser has proven itself to be a more appropriate home for web design, and CSS has come a long way to now supporting just about any effect you can pull of in Photoshop. Theoretically, we could kill Photoshop and use code 100 percent of the time. The reality is that many of us have difficulty overcoming how code is a layer abstracted from the direct manipulation we loved in Photoshop. The result is our designs look boxy and bland and are often hard to distinguish from the rest of the industry.

2 Cups Browser, 1 Cup Photoshop

Direct manipulation makes Photoshop a great environment for ideation, but the browser is the rightful home for executing and implementing the majority of our design decisions and, more importantly, testing and evaluating them. Using one entity in moderation can help overcome where the other falls short. There's no longer a clear division between the "Photoshop phase" and the "development phase." For efficiency and accuracy, it's imperative we weave between both environments as needed.

Vetting Direction Efficiently Is Critical

What worked in doing three full-page comps was that it provided a semblance of choice between distinct directions. Though we aim to be agile and flexible, exploring multiple directions is still valuable. Exercises such as moodboards and visual inventories help bring our project teams into the process of defining the most appropriate direction up front so we can continually refine as we work toward a finished site

Style Can Be Established Through Small Exercises

Full-page comps were a bear to create, especially if we tried to show multiple pages at multiple sizes. Rarely does a footer or ad block inspire the entire direction of a site, so why figure out the pixel-perfect details now? Instead, exploration through style tiles, style prototypes, and element collages help establish style without needing to define such minutiae (see **Figure 12.1**). Better yet, they help us frame the style of an entire system rather than a specific page.

Figure 12.1 Element collages are instrumental to efficient style exploration. **SOURCE:** MATT SMITH

Page-Building Is Easier with Component-Based Systems

While it's true that we're eventually implementing pages in web design, focusing on the design and style specifications for a homepage often causes us to ignore those for interior pages. The propensity to "one-off" a component to fit the page is fairly high, which can contribute to an inconsistent experience across the site. By establishing components prior to pages, we collect all the Legos we'll need for building castles, cars, and pretty much anything else we'll ever need.

Page Layers Makes Going from HTML to Photoshop Simple

Getting stuck in CSS is fairly common for most designers. Staring at code isn't the best way to breed creativity and ingenuity. Although we don't have page comps to revert to, we can take chunks or entire pages from the browser back into a fully layered PSD with Page Layers (see **Figure 12.2**). Some quick "sketching" from there should help us think through unique solutions rather than rely on ones we're used to executing through code.

Figure 12.2 Page Layers provides a way to get rendered code into Photoshop.

New Extraction Tools Get Us Back to the Browser Quicker

If we're continually going back and forth between Photoshop and the browser, we can't stumble getting in and out of either. Page Layers helps us go from HTML to PSD, but until recently there was no quick way to export our artwork. Photoshop CC has introduced two great features called Generator and Extract Assets to address this pain point, and Extract in the browser can help developers glean top-level style information without ever needing to open Photoshop.

We Can Customize Photoshop for RWD with Useful Third-Party Extensions

When we get used to a particular workflow, it's easy to accept things as they are and not be aware of the potential time-saving tools that take a little digging to unearth. Through the help of clever third-party extensions, you can build a customized Photoshop that addresses the majority of our pain points, including some of the RWD-specific ones we're discovering every day.

A Little Etiquette Goes a Long Way

No matter how slick we are individually in Photoshop, disorganization and a lack of consideration to others on our team might be crippling our workflows. With all of the moving pieces in a responsive workflow, clarity in our artwork should never be an issue since we can control it fairly easily. Naming layers, being nondestructive with our images, and wrangling type decisions can help PSD inheritors get in and out of your work in no time.

On Adoption

The first major design conference I attended was Future of Web Design NYC 2011. I traveled with my creative director and front-end developer, and the ideas shared on stage were so mind-blowing that they produced copious amounts of excitement among the three of us. In fact, we spent the car ride back up to Syracuse engaged in nonstop plotting about all the things we vowed to change in our current process, which we were all in agreement about.

We got back to work that Monday chomping at the bit, ready to share what we'd learned through the lens of "Here are all the things we need to start doing." I vividly recall the first companywide meeting being well-received, so we held another one a week later on changing how we wireframe and prototype. What we didn't expect was that a few people were so agitated that we wanted to change how they did things that they stormed out of the room not even halfway through the meeting.

I say this not to temper your excitement about visual inventories or element collages but to warn you that radical process changes aren't always popular internally and externally. It's critical that you *don't* lose your excitement for experimenting with new workflows, but driving change is going to take more than a few efforts to make happen.

TIP Don't go it alone if you don't have to. Pushing for organizational and/ or process change is a task best suited for groups. Sometimes, finding just one other advocate can help establish credibility for your claim, while also creating a sense of accountability for both of you to keep the momentum going. Try finding a co-worker or colleague who can help you assess and challenge new workflow strategies so you'll be prepared to convince others.

When we talk about transforming your process from full-page comps to designing in the browser and element collages, take a moment and realize how many facets of your current workflow and organization that new approach will affect: You need to bill differently. You need to adjust project timelines. You need to bring developers in earlier and keep designers on later. Tinkering with your business model or your company's can be difficult.

These aren't subtle shifts. These are major considerations, most of which take time to facilitate. If you don't find they're worth it in the end, you will have done a lot of reshuffling for not much return on investment.

While it's easier to suggest change when a process is completely broken, most design teams have processes that are adequate but in need of better efficiency. The sell can be a hard one, but it's rewarding if you care about designing responsively.

Strategies for Getting Buy-in Internally

Before you can illustrate the effectiveness of moodboards or style prototypes to your clients, you need to be sold on them internally. Your job as Chief Workflow Transformer is to present a compelling case to the people you work with. If you work on your own, you'll still want to be sure you're thoroughly convinced (which I hope you are).

Here are some effective methods for obtaining buy-in within your company.

Give Presentations

A good sell rarely starts with disclaimers or stating reasons for concern. You need to start with the good stuff, the stuff that convinced you in the first place. You may not be the best presenter or think you have an audience for this material, but trust me, you do (see **Figure 12.3**).

Figure 12.3 Don't be shy about sharing your passion for the transforming process.

Start by putting together a presentation. Use whatever tool you're most comfortable with; for me, it's Keynote. One of the most effective ways I've found to drive home the need for a better process is to weave back and forth between pain points and remedies. The tone you want to establish isn't "Here are all the things we do wrong, and here's how to do them right." Rather, you want something more along the lines of "Here are some areas we can be even more efficient in, and here are some ways to get there." Nobody responds well when they feel like they're being attacked, so try to convey your message as helping rather than criticizing.

In any case, presenting organized material to your team should alert them that you're serious about this making some change.

Set Realistic Expectations

After delivering the goods, it's worthwhile to convey that you don't expect changes overnight. You shouldn't; there's still a lot of figuring out to do even if everyone is on board. In a waterfall process where a designer produces comps and hands them off to a developer, the roles and their timing are clear. In a process where we jump back and forth between the browser and Photoshop, the monthly hand-offs change to daily conversations that require a little ideation, some development, and testing. That makes an impact on everyone's daily schedules and routines.

Recommended Presentations on Style

Team members are typically willing to try new methods to address workflow problems as long as they can see proof of concept. Some Googling for success stories and examples of style exploration techniques should give you enough content to lean on. If articles and pictures fail to paint a convincing picture, consider showing excerpts of conference presentations during lunch. Here are a few I recommend:

▶ Atomic Design by Brad Frost (*www.vimeo.com/109130093*)

▶ Evolving the Digital Style Guide by Andy Pratt (*www.vimeo.com/ 95268339*)

▶ Get Your Visual Style On by Yesenia Perez-Cruz, Ben Callahan, and Dan Mall (*www.vimeo.com/89535833*)

▶ Prototyping Style by Ben Callahan (*www.vimeo.com/71354748*)

▶ Clandestine Photoshop by Dan Rose (*www.vimeo.com/106070388*; I'm recommending mine only because it maps the closest to the contents of this book)

I heard of one design agency that, upon adopting a new responsive process, restructured their office. Since the traditional divide between designers and developers creates inefficiencies when going from idea to code, they sat developers next to designers. The thinking was that if both parties were in better proximity to one another, they would find it easier to tackle responsive issues from both angles instead of one and then the other.

It's prudent to have a group discussion about potential concerns before jumping into a completely restructured workflow (see **Figure 12.4**): *How will we bill for this? Will anyone's roles change? How quickly can we make a visual inventory?* All of these questions can't be resolved without some trial and error, but the hope is that understanding that it'll take a bit of figuring out should disarm anyone from stating that it's not possible. It's your job to communicate why it's worth it.

Work the Food Chain

Begin by presenting your new RWD methods to the people with whom you work most directly. You want to get buy-in from the people in roles most similar to yours. In doing so, you create allies for trying to convince bigger fish in your organization. Failure to get fellow designers and developers on board before approaching C-level folks means you run the risk of alienating your colleagues, who may not be on board with everything you present.

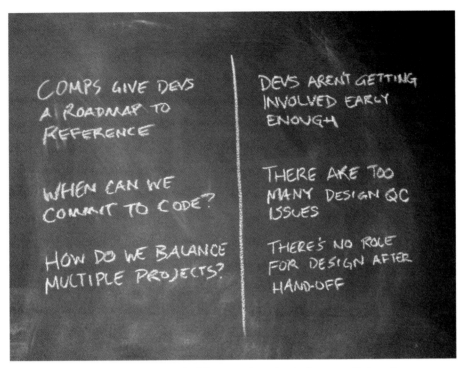

Figure 12.4 Have a round-table discussion about the pros and cons to adopting new methods, and encourage everyone to voice any concerns.

With a small group of supporters established, refine and tailor your presentation to others. They may have different interests than designers, so address those. For instance, it may be worth highlighting how a new workflow would facilitate better client communication.

Attend Conferences

It's hard to argue with anyone who is up-to-date, and almost everyone respects those who willingly seek learning opportunities such as those found at industry conferences. You won't return as an expert on all aspects of design, but attending conferences establishes you as connected to the design community. There's authority in that.

When you make workflow pitches and presentations, stating examples and insight from conferences goes a long way in establishing objective credibility (see **Figure 12.5** on the next page). If you can describe best practices used successfully by designers elsewhere, your audience will be less likely to regard your pitch as completely subjective. Attend conferences as often as you can, and report back to your team how other designers are tackling the same problems you have.

Figure 12.5 Design conferences offer tons of firsthand examples of transformed workflows.

You want your team excited to try a few new things. Openly discuss the merits of various approaches and workflow tweaks to get everyone on board and advocating for change. You're looking for unbridled enthusiasm, not passive agreement.

Strategies for External Getting Buy-In

Once you have buy-in from the team, it's time to reach out to your clients and stakeholders, who likely haven't ever dealt with anything outside of receiving three full-page comps for sign-off. Don't underestimate this fact: Your customer may take pride in equating this traditional approach with how web design works. Making your pitch successful may require some rewiring and education.

Reset Expectations

When I got my driveway installed, I had only one point of reference for how it was typically done and was reluctant to take the contractor at his word when he suggested paving it in two phases instead of all at once. He said this isn't how everyone does it, or even how he's always done it, but he's found that it produces a driveway that lasts longer. Up to this point, I had always thought paving a driveway was simple: You pour some asphalt down, smooth it, and walk away forever. According to my contractor, this approach is problematic.

It's highly possible that he duped me. What he did establish, however, is that he's the expert and has a reason for doing something I might not be familiar with. I respect that and feel our design clients do as well. Visual inventories and component libraries aren't familiar to them, but if we sell the value of their role in a responsive project, we have decent odds of convincing them to abandon the comp approach they likely experienced last time they had their site redesigned.

Outlining the timing and role of every exercise in your new process goes a long way toward gaining the trust of your client. If you substitute element collages for full-page comps without giving them any warning, they'll probably be confused as to what they are and why they help the process. Start by providing a road map of every design conversation you plan on having from project kickoff to project delivery.

Increase Communication and Involvement

As you learned in Chapters 5 and 6, bringing your clients and stakeholders into the design process can be a foreign concept if you're used to presenting work for approval. But it's an effective approach, and I'd even argue a necessary one for a responsive workflow; you need their input for design direction and decisions throughout the entire process, so it doesn't make sense to work in a silo between milestones.

Providing opportunities for clients to be involved will help you get external buy-in to a new process. If your clients continually feel like a valued part of finding the solution—which they should be—they'll be less resistant to trying new methods. When they try to cling to traditional approaches, present them with the option of contributing to the success of a new method: *We'd love to try style tiles because they'll get us into a direction more quickly. Would you mind helping us find a few viable approaches?* This should get them excited to participate.

TIP Don't be afraid to engage your clients with exercises similar to the ones we designers use. Sketching sessions, however rough, can help clients communicate their perspectives in terms you're familiar with, especially if their industry may not be so familiar to you.

When framed as an attempt to stay on top of the increasingly moving target the Web has become, new approaches and the opportunity to contribute to them should appeal to both us and the ones we work for.

Affirm Where Things Are Going

A traditional process has clear objectives for its deliverables. A design comp leads to an HTML & CSS rendering, which leads to a CMS implementation. Relying on small exercises to define design direction and style exploration can make it harder to see where all of it is going.

One of the best ways to curb frustration is to continually set up what you've done so far, what you're currently doing, and how it will impact the next part of the project. For example, "Last time, we had a great conversation about some viable directions to explore looking at the visual inventory. We've taken that input and crafted some element collages to discuss today. This discussion will help us continue to define the course we're on and determine what styles are most appropriate moving forward when we produce high-fidelity prototypes of a few templates to review."

Communicate with your clients and stakeholders how the input they supply helps shape the direction of each exercise. Set a framework for the kind of feedback you'll need for the next step.

What Happens When Things Go Wrong

Just because any of the strategies in this book seem better than comps doesn't mean they're safe from trouble. The next few sections describe some of the heavier issues that might arise.

The Client Can't Settle on a Direction

If your client responds to every visual inventory characteristic or element collage exploration with "That seems like it would work," the root cause can be hard to nail down. Yes, you may have presented some stunning options and made it an objectively difficult decision to start paring down, but it's also possible you haven't given them not enough differentiation between the options.

It's OK if two directions are determined to be viable in a visual inventory. Go forth and explore them. However, you should be able to pit the advantages of one against the other the clearer the directions come into view: *Do you think your users will appreciate the active color palette's connection to your logo?* Asking critical questions about each direction may help your client articulate how appropriate each one is.

Remember, your client is an expert in their field just as you are in yours. Try asking questions that require them to lean on their knowledge of their customer base. With their customers in mind, it may be easier to vet which direction is more appropriate.

The Element Collage Misses the Mark Entirely

Just like full-page comps, the execution of element collages has the potential to fall short of client expectations. Try not to get stuck in a loop of editing an element collage based on requests like "Change the blue to red, and bring the header up a little bit." This kind of feedback won't allow a direction to evolve; it just communicates to a client that they have the authority to make specific design edits.

Instead, poor input received from a moodboard or visual inventory could be the root cause. Don't blame your client. It could be a product of poor questions on your part. In any event, revisit what was established in these conversations again to ensure you're on the right track. Then, pair the feedback against what you explored in Photoshop. If you're missing the mark on execution, ask your client to better articulate what it is that doesn't align like they hoped.

Should you need to drastically adjust an element collage, take solace in the fact that doing so takes only a fraction of the time full-page mockups do. Trashing a 20-hour comp leads to much misery. Trashing a six-hour element collage, while not ideal, is still a relatively small course of action to get back on track.

Designer/Developer Discord Still Exists

Involving developers earlier and designers later isn't always going to result in everyone singing "Kumbaya." Frustrations with designers not understanding how code works and developers not being able to color their way out of a wet paper bag may still exist after you thought uniting everyone on a new workflow was a good thing. Don't worry, it was; but fostering effective designer/developer communication is a whole other animal.

Etiquette will help, as will more frequent interactions and conversations. The hope is that both of these will give you an opportunity for better understanding of design and development techniques and methodologies. You'll reach true harmony when you succeed in blurring the line between which person is capable of doing what. A designer who codes effectively and a developer capable of making intelligent design decisions make for a powerful team, but don't expect it to happen overnight if it doesn't already exist. It'll come.

Adjusting Your Perspective on Tools

In writing this book, I've experienced an epiphany of sorts about Photoshop in a responsive process. It's hard to justify keeping it around, though I'd like to believe I've made a strong case for doing so, and I hope I've helped you see how advantage it is to do so. Even so, tools that aim to replace it will continue to come.

My advice is to continue to entertain such alternatives because staying open at this juncture of the Web's evolution is essential to keeping up with it. But you should also assess *how* you use your tools as viable alternatives.

Repurposing Tools May Be Better Than Getting New Ones

With new tools and techniques popping up seemingly every day, there has never been a better time to assess the tools and techniques you currently employ. It may take turning Photoshop and how you use it on its head, but the result is that it addresses RWD process pain points in ways that other tools can't—for me, anyway.

Those words, "for me," are critical to adopting a successful responsive workflow. There's no single approach that stands above the others for everyone because the situations, clients, and projects a designer encounters can vary so greatly. Find what works for you, share it, and continually improve on it.

To move web design forward, you need to ask the question, "How can I use the tools I have to solve this problem?" rather than, "What tool solves all of the problems I have?" The distinction is crucial to being innovative or simply chasing the newest app of the week.

Train yourself to be a critical thinker, a professional interrogator, and a problem solver. Allow your process to reflect that. In doing so, you'll find our friend Photoshop to be of great use, and the more unconventionally you use it, the better it will serve you.

Index